HEaling hurts

by
Minister Patricia Jones, MA/ICADC

1663 LIBERTY DRIVE, SUITE 200
BLOOMINGTON, INDIANA 47403
(800) 839-8640
WWW.AUTHORHOUSE.COM

First published by AuthorHouse 06/03/05

ISBN: 1-4208-5393-7 (sc)

Printed in the United States of America
Bloomington, Indiana

This book is printed on acid-free paper.

DEDICATION

I dedicate HEALING HURTS to my God as "praise" to Him, who loved me enough to make a way out of hell for me. I thank God for believing enough in me to complete this task.

Thank you, Daddy. I love you!

ACKNOWLEDGMENTS

To those people who believed in me during this process, I owe my deepest thanks. I give my thanks to all my friends and family who gave financial contributions and encouraging words to make this book a reality. I couldn't dare list them all.

I thank my friend Marsha Lewis for her encouragement and editing. I give my thanks to Steven Forshee for his help with the cover of this book and seeing the vision. I thank my granddaughter Kambre for always encouraging me by asking about the book. I give my sincere thanks to my friend Diane Yamamoto for her contribution and her faith in God. I thank my husband Steven Jones for believing in my vision and the cold drinks he would bring to me as I worked away on this book. I have to acknowledge my mother, Ruby Taylor, my brothers, Humphrey, Duck, Kenneth, and Timmy. I am so proud of my children, Sookie, Julia, Marcus, and Sophia, who gave me wonderful grandchildren, Andre, Kambre, Sissy, Marcus, Isaiah, Mya, Michael, and Jeremiah. I love you all very much!

Last but certainly not least, I have a deep gratitude and thanks to Pastors Ronald and Wilma Scott for their teaching and encouragement. They have been supportive of me through some of the most difficult times in my life. Their teaching has given me the enthusiasm and wisdom to step out and be what God has called me to be. This book is my praise to God and my way of passing what I have been given on to the world.

INTRODUCTION
TO HEALING HURTS

HEALING HURTS is a book of events from my life story that cover the hurt, pain, and suffering it takes to heal. HEALING HURTS is a twofold message of God's power. In one aspect, it displays the fact that God heals our hurts, and secondly, it exhibits the fact that it hurts to heal. Have you ever asked God, "Why so much pain?" Well, I have, and there hasn't been just one answer to that question; there are many reasons.

This book covers my drug addiction and other struggles I have found myself in. It also includes my recovery, which addresses the reality of life and healing. Healing has a great deal to do with changing the way we think and the way we act. Sometimes this can be a painful process, and the process of healing can last a lifetime. It is a process we have to surrender to in order to win. The apostle Paul made mention of pressing toward the mark of the High Calling, which is a process of restoration and healing. During our lives, we strive to be better people by using the Lord Jesus as our perfect example. Through all our trials and struggles of life, we are learning how to live.

Out of my hurt, God put a ministry inside of me called "HEALING HURTS MINISTRY," which shows others that we overcome by the blood of Jesus and the word of our testimony. I hope by reading this book that you will be able to see the distance that God brought me. I was a suffering drug addict, and I am now a licensed minister of the Gospel and a substance abuse counselor, called by God to reach out to suffering women and suffering people just like myself to offer hope where there is none. I have dedicated my life to helping others heal from their addictions and their pasts.

I believe that because of God's deliverance in my life and my relationship with Jesus Christ, it has given me the power to raise the dead! The power to raise the dead is simply the love of God that lives in us. This power enables us to speak life and deliverance into someone else's life as well as our own. Through my experience in counseling hard-to-reach people, like drug addicts and people incarcerated, I have seen "love" change the hardest hearts; it changed mine. I can say that I am an "overcomer" today. I believe that people who make the major difference in the lives of others are not so much the ones with many credentials, but people with the greatest concern for God's purpose and His people. When we go through the pains and struggles in life, we develop empathy, which is a concern and love for those going though the same struggles.

HEALING HURTS is a book of hopes and truths that can set you free from the bondage that has held you back for so long. We are to be free from the burdens of this world. Jesus came into this world that we might have life and have it more abundantly—meaning abundant peace, joy, health, and finances—plus to live a life that is rich and free! And through His giving, Jesus felt "pain" and "hurt" in order for the world to experience healing. When He went to the cross, He felt every <u>blow</u> and every <u>word</u> that came to Him. And these are the stripes that heal us. With every painful stripe put on His body flowed the blood that heals us today. Even more, before the cross, Jesus went about the earth "HEALING HURTS." He was known for healing the hurts of the people, and He is still known today and forever more to be our "*Healing.*" The word of God deals with healing the "person" to healing the "land."

The words "HEALING HURTS" was such a powerful message for me when I heard it. I need to thank a little girl for the title of my book. Several years ago, after finishing a workout at a local fitness center, a little girl was in the dressing room next to mine crying, and I could hear her mother trying to comfort her. I didn't get a chance to meet her or see what she looked like, but I heard her. What I do know is that the Holy Spirit spoke to me through her. As I listened, I could hear through the wall her crying. I thought, "Well, maybe she fell and hurt herself." I could hear her mother in a loving and consoling way offering a remedy to her daughter's pain. She offered to put a Band-Aid on the "hurt" and told her daughter, "This will help it to *heal.*" (How many times have we been offered a Band-Aid to cover our hurts? And how many times have we symbolically tried to cover our hurts and brokenness with a Band-Aid method?)

Well, in the midst of her crying and *pain*, it appeared she wanted something a little faster or an easier, softer way. The little girl responded to her mother's gestures by saying in a panicky, loud, terrified voice, "Mommy! No! No! No! I don't want to heal because HEALING HURTS!" At that moment, my life seemed to flash before me, and I had to sit down and think about what I just heard. I knew based on the tribulations of my life that God Himself had just spoken to me. I knew that I had refused to heal from my damaged emotions that kept me using drugs and alcohol, because I was afraid of the pain. I just wanted it to go away. What a revelation in the words this small girl spoke in fear, "HEALING HURTS!" We often sound like this little girl when we talk to God in our fear: "No, God, it might hurt!" I too have been afraid to heal.

So many times in our lives, we have avoided healing because it is too painful to go through. Many avoid their past hurts because it is too painful to look at, and it is easier to medicate with drugs, sex, food, or some other addictive habit. In order to get over a painful or hurtful situation in life, we have to be healed. In fact, to clean up the wreckage from the past, it may hurt. Sometimes it seems easier to stay in a bad situation than to come out due to the fear of the pain involved in the healing process to change. We are people living in the "instant-gratification world." If it doesn't have a remote to it, it's considered to be of low value. We want what we want when we want it. We expect to learn patience instantly or in a hurry and look for the magical cure. We want instant relief from *pain*, and don't dare talk to us about a process. We have to be willing to go through the process of healing and "HEALING HURTS"; whether you are considered good or bad, HEALING HURTS! Rich or poor, HEALING HURTS! Black or white, HEALING HURTS!

Healing from my drug addiction has been a process of restoration and repair. I was broken, and I needed to be repaired by the One who made me. Think about it; would it be a wise decision to take your custom-made car to the dealer that made it for repairs and maintenance or to have some shade-tree mechanic do the work to avoid some of the painful cost? If you take it to the one who made it and knows all the parts and specializes in its custom build, the results would be a perfect job well done. Well, it's the same with us; it would be smarter for us to put all our hurts in the hand of our Creator and Maker. He is the One who knows everything about us, and He has so gently and delicately made each and every one of us. Plus, God knows what we need to *heal.* Our healing process is not on us; it is on God, and it's done on His time.

Healing is a mending process to repair what is broken. For example, when a surgeon goes in to operate, he mends the brokenness and prepares you for the healing process. No healing process is without pain; therefore, one of the first things the doctor offers is a pain medication to help ease the process of healing. After the pain and healing is over, change has taken place, in some circumstances to appear brand new. God Himself is in the restoration business, redeeming, rebuilding, restoring, refining, and renewing our lives. We are in the operating room, and He is the chief surgeon.

The definition of healing is to become or make one well. It means to prosper and live well or become healthier. Healing is to mend, to cure or remedy, and a method to restore to health. Healing is to repair, to make better or reform. According to Matthew 14:34–36, all who touched Jesus were healed. When we touch Jesus, we are made new, and old things pass away. God's desire is that we prosper and be in good health; **this is to be healed**. I am sure we all have room for some type of **healing** in our lives.

We realize that HEALING HURTS, and "hurts" can be physical pain, mental pain, or suffering, damage, or harm. But this particular "hurts" suggests **that the pain and suffering are without serious impairment. (For example, the drill used by a dentist may hurt or cause temporary pain, but it does not injure.)**

1 Samuel 10:6–7 says that when the Spirit of the Lord comes upon you with power, you will be changed into a different person. The wonderful thing about healing is that the end is better than the beginning. Take for example the story of Job in the Bible. Job did not know it would be, but his later life was better than the beginning. Job suffered massive and incredible losses, and he too had something to learn through his suffering and his healing. We don't want to hurt, but when our Savior was on the cross, He was hurting. He hurt for our healing. He took all our hurts and pain to the cross with Him.

We have to go through something in order to be delivered. When I accepted Jesus Christ as my Lord and Savior, I was accepted into the family of God. I received my entrance into Glory and all the inheritance of our Lord and Savior, Jesus. In addition, I received His suffering; now, what does that mean? Before there can be a resurrection, there has to be a death. Most of us are afraid to die because it just **looks** like it **hurts** like hell! Well, Jesus had to die a horrible death in order to live and that we may also live. He suffered for our sake, and we will also suffer.

During the healing process, we have many questions as Job had, but those who are willing to work through the pain, to walk it out and seek God for healing, can find the answers. Similar to Job, there were times during my addiction that I just wanted to die. Job suffered so much pain that he said, *"If my sadness could be weighed and my troubles be put on the scales, they would be heavier than all the sands of the sea ... Oh, that I might have my request, that God would grant my hope. I wish he would crush me. I wish he would reach out his hand and kill me ... I do not have the strength to endure. I do not have a goal that encourages me to carry on. Do I have strength as hard as stone? Is my body made of bronze? No, I am utterly helpless, without any chance of success" (Job 6:2–3, 8–9, 11– 13; New Living Bible Version)*. He was in the midst of a healing process. There has to be some type of loss before there can be healing. Job could not see that his life was going to be completely healed from all the pain and loss, and sometimes neither can we.

It was not so much the loss of the possessions that made Job cry out to God, because his self-esteem was not tied up in what he had. It was the pain he had to go through to reach his healing that caused Job to cry out. Like Job, my pain caused me to cry out in my despair, to cry out to whatever was there. I didn't have a relationship with God at the time, although I believed He existed. If you have never cried out to God before, you can, and He will hear you! He is that kind of God. Pain will cause you to cry out as the little girl did in the stall next to mine. When we cry out, God can and will hear us, and He is so loving and caring. He takes us in his loving arms and aids our pain as the mother did for her daughter and as you would do for your own crying and hurting child. God is our refuge and our strength when we are in the storms of life; He will never leave us or forsake us. I know that God has something to say, so remain open-minded as you read, receive what God is saying to you. God is so powerful that He can use one word to change your life. Say to yourself, **"Self, there is a word in this book for me."**

I pray that while you read this book and go through my healing process, you will come to know the Lord Jesus Christ as your personal Savior and that you will come to know Him as I did. Most of all, you will start to build an intimate relationship with Him, and if you already know Him, I hope that your love will grow for Him even more.

My prayer for this book: I pray that this book will reach out and pull the drug addict out of the streets of drugs and the bondage of addiction. I pray that it will reach and touch the hearts of denial and open the door to a new start. I pray in the name of Jesus that this book will reach somebody's pain to let him or her know healing is available. I pray that the words of this book will touch somebody's cry for help, for there is a new way of living. I pray that these words will touch somebody's struggle to live life on life's terms. We need each other, and I pray this book will touch somebody as God has touched me.

I pray that the spirit of God will move as you read this book, to inspire change, repentance, deliverance, and salvation. **I want to write about God in such a way that it will reveal His Glory to you.** *This book is my praise to God!*

Whatever your need may be, I know a God that can meet you on your level, in your situation, and in your circumstance. I pray that if you are not saved that you will stop now and ask Jesus Christ to come into your life to be your Lord and Savior. In Jesus' name I ask these things, Amen. If God can save me, there is hope for any and everybody!

TABLE OF CONTENTS

CHAPTER ONE
"IDENTIFYING AND ADMITTING THE PROBLEM"

"I CAN'T DO IT BY MYSELF"

"Each time he said, 'My gracious favor is all you need. My power works best in your weakness.' So now I am glad to boast about my weaknesses, so that the power of Christ may work through me" (2 Cor. 12:9).

Hi! My name is Trish, and I am a recovering addict, and I thank God for the twelve-step support groups. If you don't understand why I use the term "recovering addict," read the book! When I say God is Good, it is not just a cliché! I mean it; He is Good! Awesome! Jehovah Jireh! Jehovah Rapher! He is my Provider and my Healer. I am excited about my God and awestruck with His power.

In March of 1988, God saved me from my alcohol and drug addiction. From that day forward, He has continued to heal my hurts and issues that lay hidden underneath my alcohol and drug abuse. I started experimenting with cigarettes at age thirteen with my cousin. I guess I displayed addictive behavior even then because the cigarettes made us sick the first time, but we didn't let that stop us. We tried smoking again and again until we got it right. This led to over twenty years of cigarette addiction for me.

I had my first drink at the age of fifteen, which was wine that my friends and I stole from the neighborhood bootlegger. The first time I used marijuana was about a year later with friends. They told me if I smoked the joint, I would laugh harder at the Richard Pryor movie. Well, it made sense to me at the time, so I tried it. It just doesn't make good sense now. My first experience with my drug of choice, cocaine, was at the age of twenty-three; it made me feel great! In my twenties, I used drugs as much as I could. I used pills, alcohol, cocaine, marijuana, speed, hashish, heroin, PCP, and other drugs I can't remember the names of because I didn't take time to ask. If it got me high, I used it!

I used cocaine and whatever drug I could get as much and as often as I could. As a matter of fact, I made drug use my career, and I set a goal to use until I was an old lady. By now, I had three children, quit my jobs, and bailed out on my responsibilities. I didn't want responsibilities because they got in the way of my drug use. My life just kept going downhill and continued to give territory to cocaine, to a point where I no longer had a choice; I had to use! Cocaine controlled my choices. I started to believe that it was my destiny to die a drug addict.

The first step to healing is admitting that there is a problem, admitting that something is wrong. When we recognize our brokenness, it opens the door for recovery. We cannot find a solution to a problem that does not exist. As painful as it may be to take a look at ourselves, we have to admit the problem. This is very difficult for some of us because it appears that we are weak if we admit to certain problems. Sometimes we are more concerned with how people see us than who we really are. So we spend a lot of time and effort pretending to be something that we are not and protecting these false images for the sake of others. We have to stop acting and performing for people and get honest before God; He is the only one that matters. To start the healing process, it takes honesty and humility to be open-minded enough to see the truth.

Identifying and admitting our problems can be much like a child trying to take his or her first steps; it can be intimidating. The child is afraid, but it is important that he or she takes the first step. So he or she falls and gets up during this process of learning how to walk, and so must we. My past life experiences, obstacles, and situations have led me down the wrong path many times. I had to accept this truth in order to move forward with my life. God has given me steps to a new life—steps that I never knew existed.

I never thought I could stop using cocaine because my addiction controlled my life. I could not see my life without being high on cocaine or some other drug. I honestly believed that I would die a junkie. I believed that this was what was meant for me, because I saw no way out. I was so powerless over this drug and my lifestyle that I was determined to do anything to get what I needed. I was trapped inside of myself, on the verge of losing myself in a world of darkness. I was dying inside of myself.

I am reminded of a time several years ago in the middle of my drug addiction, locked in a hotel room with a lifelong friend. He was shooting cocaine in his arm with a needle that had become very dull, and I was smoking cocaine on a pipe. I had never tried the needle before because of my phobia of needles, but there I was watching one of the grossest things I had ever seen, the blood and the mess of getting high intravenously. I was in the very core of my insanity and inability to stop this downhill run I was on. I started to contemplate, "Well, maybe if I shut my eyes and turn my head, I can allow him to shoot me up with this dirty, dull needle in an attempt to get higher." I was too far gone. Although I didn't try it, my thinking was deteriorating at this time.

I struggled for many years. I felt I was two different people; one part of me wanted to quit, and another part of me could not quit. I realized that something other than me was controlling me; something had taken over my body, my thinking, and my senses. I would decide on many days that it would be the day that I would quit only to fail again. Each morning, I would make a promise to myself, and by noon, I would be high on crack cocaine again, feeling completely hopeless to stop this deadly cycle. The apostle Paul said the words, "I want to do right but there is something inside of me that won't let me."

In my powerlessness to stop my addiction or mange my own life, I returned home one day from a cocaine binge. I was in the bed most of the day, until my five-year-old son became frightened enough or tired enough to come into my room. He came to my bedside and said, "Mama, I am just a little boy, and I cannot take care of this house by myself." That's when I knew I was out of control. The comment cut me so deeply but not bad enough to quit. I continued with my drug addiction, maybe even using more to cover the pain, shame, and guilt of my using. As I write about this, it brings sorrow to my heart and tears to my eyes to wonder what fear my son was experiencing.

I was sick, and I suffered from the disease of addiction. I know now that addiction is not only a physical, emotional, and compulsive obsession; it is a spirit, a disease. (Some will disagree, but that is perfectly all right with me.) Addiction is a disease that separated me from the peace of God, and a disease is a spirit. What do I mean by that? In the book of Ephesians, the apostle Paul says that we do not fight against flesh and blood but against spirits in the unseen world.

A disease is a spirit that needs a body to function, to have life, or power. The disease of diabetes needs a body, cancer needs a body, HIV needs a body; if it has no body, then it has no power! A spirit needs a body. Alcohol and drugs have absolutely no power until I ingest them into my body. A disease cannot be seen with the natural eye, neither can a spirit. Addiction, alcoholism, cancer, diabetes, etc. cannot be seen with the natural eye; we can only see the effects of the disease within the body. We can look at a person and see the physical, emotional, and social affects of a disease, but can you see the disease itself? No! It needs a body!

When my eyes were opened, I came to the awareness of what I had been doing to myself. I noticed that most liquor stores advertise wine and "spirits." I have been tempted to walk in a liquor store and ask to purchase a spirit only to get the response. Our bodies are temples that belong to

God. My God, what have we been buying and putting into our temples with very little thought or concern. We are to offer our bodies as a living sacrifice that is holy and pleasing to God, not full of wine and drugs.

I can recall in the late stages of my addiction to cocaine that I found myself alone most of the time getting high and watching the television. It is amazing that the only thing I remember from those days on the television was a preacher. It appeared to be a set up that I always caught the part when he was saying with all the strength and power of the Holy Spirit, **"Don't just sit there; do something with your life!"** That statement would cut right through me like a double-edged sword, because I was doing exactly "nothing" with my life!

One day while isolated in my home, smoking cocaine, this same preacher came on the television, and I knew he was going to say those terrible words, **"Don't just sit there; do something with your life!"** I tried to beat him to the punch so I hurried to the television to turn it down before the words could roll off his lips, and I tripped over a footstool and fell right in front of the television, but I made it! I turned the volume down and lay there on the floor in front of the television and read his lips, **"Don't just sit there; do something with your life!"** Oh! It sounded louder and cut deeper than ever. How disgusted I felt. I cried from the bottom of my soul. I knew something had to happen, and I needed help. Now the insanity is that after this soul-wrenching cry, I continued to use drugs and had no power to quit. I would pray and long for God to allow the authorities to bust me, that maybe a jail sentence would stop me. I believed at the time that it would be the only way I could stop my cycle of addiction.

The day came when I hit a bottom in my life and there was nowhere else to go; I saw death. After a few days of smoking crack cocaine, I was walking through the house, and I passed a mirror. I had been avoiding mirrors because I didn't want to see what was really going on. I took a look at myself in the mirror, and I saw death, and I asked God, "Where did I go?" Now, I knew I was looking at myself in the mirror, but what I saw as I looked at my reflection in the mirror was not familiar to me. I could not recognize myself. I could not identify my own body. I was trapped inside of myself with no way out. What a scary place it was for me, a place where most people give up hope and die or go completely insane. God found me and pulled me out of the **dungeon** of my soul and gave me a "New Hope."

What a life-changing moment. I weighed approximately ninety-five pounds from the constant use of cocaine, and I was in physical, mental, and spiritual pain. In February 1988, I recall getting on my knees next to my bed about three o'clock in the morning wrapped in pain, high as

I could be on cocaine. I cried out to God, "Please help me; I can't stop; don't let me die like this!" Much like Peter, in his desperation, he cried out to Christ when he was sinking on the water, and Jesus immediately reached down to save him so he would not drown. Jesus reached down in the depths of my insanity and pulled me out of the bottom of my addiction. I thought I would die a drug addict, but Mercy and Grace said, "No!" I was drowning, and I had given up all hope to survive. **2 Corinthians 1:8–10,** *"I think you ought to know, dear brothers and sisters, about the trouble we went through in the province of Asia. We were crushed and completely overwhelmed, and we thought we would never live through it. In fact, we expected to die but as a result, we learned not to rely on ourselves, but on God who can raise the dead."*

Sometimes all it takes is an honest cry for help. When I cried out to God from the bottom of my pain and addiction, it was not with some fancy prayer; it was just a sincere, "God, please help me!"

God intervened in my active drug addiction by using my dope-dealing boyfriend to direct me to a treatment center. My grandmother would always say, "The Lord moves in mysterious ways." Well, she was right! Subsequently, after I cried out to God for help, my boyfriend volunteered information about rehabilitation. I knew absolutely nothing about where to seek help. I know now that it was the direction of the Holy Spirit. My boyfriend's plan was to become rich by selling cocaine, and he figured if I could stop using up all the profit, the faster it would happen. He really hadn't planned on all the changes that took place after I stopped using drugs. One of those changes included me making the decision that I deserved better than the way I was living with him, and that brought on changes that did not include him.

My desire today is to offer hope to the hopeless and answer somebody else's cry for help. I thank God that I did not die in my misery or end up totally insane. *"Death had its hands around my throat; the terrors of the grave overtook me. I saw only trouble and sorrow. [I thought I would die a drug addict.] Then I called on the name of the Lord: 'Please Lord, save me!' I was facing death and then He saved me. Now I can rest again for the Lord has been so good to me. He saved me from death. I will not die, but I will live to tell what the Lord has done!"* (taken from Ps. 116:3, 4, 6, 7, 8; New Living). Our God has power over death, so death can't hold us. Through Christ we are offered an eternal healing.

I came face to face with the door of healing in my life, and all I had to do was open it and go through. I had to admit that my lifestyle had separated me from God. Actually, I had exhausted my entire life putting things before God, and this caused the separation that made my life totally chaotic.

When I confessed with my mouth and took the risk, it opened the door to my healing process and the process of restoration. I had to tell somebody that I had a problem and I needed help. The word of God says to confess our sins one to another that we may be healed. I realized at this point that everything I had tried to fix my own life with had failed. The drugs, food, sex, money, relationships, men, marriages, fast life, cars, clothing, etc., they all failed to fill the emptiness or hunger inside of me for any length of time. All of these fixes were only temporary. These things were little gods in my life with no lasting power to satisfy me. The bottom line is that they do not work as they should; they are only instant gratifications that last for only a moment. I found myself sacrificing everything for that moment of instant feel-good or pleasure.

Not only that, my drug had become everything to me; I gave up a normal life and stooped to an animal level of living. I know what's meant by it's a "dog-eat-dog world." There are so many horrible and unusual things happening in these days and times, especially to obtain drugs. We have so many storms in our lives. I know that someone reading this book is having some type of storm in his or her life or getting ready to enter into one or coming out of one. My pastor says that if you live long enough, you will have a storm. Many times we cause our own storms by the choices we make. Our storms represent trouble or trials we are faced with.

This book will reach those who are suffering from a broken heart, imprisoned to some type of fleshly desire, mourning some type of loss (such as divorce, death of a loved one, job, or home), suffering a bad marriage, owing bills that are piling up, and/or prisoners to sin, drugs, sex, alcohol, and money. The storm is raging, and you are going down. Thank God that the door opens to healing when we can identify the storm, which is the problem.

My drug use and lifestyle took the place of my children, my family, my God, and my lover; actually, it was the most important thing in my life. So when I admitted that I had a problem to start the process of healing, I had to give up my drug, and to me that was like giving up my world. So this decision left me feeling totally empty, out there on a limb and wondering, "What do I do now? What happens now? I'm hurting so bad."

Proverbs 23:29–35 describes alcoholism and addiction pretty clearly: *"Who has anguish? Who has sorrow? Who is always fighting? Who is always complaining? Who has unnecessary bruises? Who has bloodshot eyes? It is the one who spends long hours in the taverns, trying out new drinks. Don't let the sparkle and smooth taste of wine deceive you. For in* *the end it bites like a poisonous serpent; it stings like a viper. You will see hallucinations, and you will say crazy things. You will stagger like a sailor tossed at sea, clinging to a swaying mast. And you will say, 'They hit me, but I didn't feel it. I didn't even know it when they beat me up. When will I wake up so I can have another drink?'"*

I had to accept my limitations, stop hiding, and admit that I was a drug addict and admit my powerlessness to heal myself. Some people have thought this statement to be a slap in God's face to admit powerlessness. The apostle Paul says in 2 Corinthians 12:10, *"In my weakness I am <u>made</u> strong."* What I realize for myself is that when I gave up the power that I thought I had, I gained power in God. I learned not to rely on myself but on God who can raise the dead, and apart from God I can do nothing. His power works best in our weakness. When we reach a point of total helplessness, we seek God differently. In Acts chapter nine, Paul's position of conversion caused him to seek God with a sincere heart. He humbled himself and his prayer life changed; his worldly knowledge could not help him in this situation. He was blind physically and spiritually, but Jesus gives sight to the blind. Paul had to be in constant prayer before the Lord, because when the Lord told Ananias to go lay hands on Paul and pray for him, the Lord said, "You will find him praying," which was a new position for Saul/Paul. Paul was seeking the one true God for his deliverance.

God gives us instructions for healing, deliverance, how to live, salvation, how to love, marriage, and prosperity. Anything we can think of has already been covered in the Bible. God gives us a way out of whatever situation we find ourselves in. So many times we need to just follow a set of simple instructions that we may be healed.

For instance, the Bible talks about Naaman in 2 Kings chapter five and how he was a powerful man in one area of his life and in the other he suffered from leprosy. Leprosy was a disease that made you an outcast in those days as addiction does in these days.

Naaman went to the man of God to be healed and found that his healing was not coming the way he had expected it to come. Sometimes in order to be healed we have to do something that we don't want to do. We may have to do something that may not make good sense to us or even to the people around us. People have been known to put God in a box by saying He only operates or moves a certain way, and by doing so, we can limit his ability to work in our lives. His thoughts are not our thoughts, and His thoughts are higher than our thoughts. Therefore, He is able to do exceedingly and abundantly above all that we can think with our minds. Our healing will not always come exactly the way the next person's will. Why is it that God heals one person from cancer miraculously and instantly, and another He may lead through the process of therapy to healing? Is He not in both healing events? Of course He is; it's still God! It's still healing!

I had been so used to being in control that the thought of admitting I had a problem made me feel humiliated. I had to become willing to sacrifice who I thought I was to find my healing. Naaman too had to realize that his healing was not in his identity, and he could not pay for his healing. He had to admit that he had no power to produce his own healing and follow a set of simple instructions. So, this admission put him in a position to be healed. To receive Jesus' help and begin recovery, we have to first recognize and admit how helpless we really are without Him. Jesus' greatest desire was reaching the so-called social outcasts (drug addicts) because they admitted their lowly, helpless positions. Jesus said, "I came in this world for the sick, not for those that think they are well." I thank God that I am sick enough for Jesus. The sicker we are, the more His glory can be seen through our healing. Many drug addicts think that they are too bad to come to the Lord. We may even try to clean up first, but Jesus wants us just as sick as we are, and He can make us well.

Sometimes we may need to hit rock bottom to realize that God's way is the only way. That's not just with drug use, but also in any area of our lives. We have to come to the end of ourselves and exhaust our own resources. The time came when I was just sick of myself and ready for something different to happen. I had to express my pain to God instead of trying to escape it. When we can admit to the problem in our lives and we have failed at trying to deal with this situation alone, it will open up the door for our healing. Sometimes we are not willing to do what needs to be done. After we identify the problem, we get into the solution.

I admitted myself to a thirty-day alcohol and drug treatment center for my drug addiction. I didn't like the words they were throwing around, words like "powerlessness," "unmanageability," and "insanity." So, I had to inform these kind people that those words did not and could not fit me because I just had a little problem with cocaine, sometimes. I failed to mention to the admissions nurse that I was smoking enough cocaine to kill a horse! I was hurting inside, and inside I was crying, *"Please don't send me away! I'll die!"* I had too much false pride to admit how serious my problem was, and I feared they would ask me to leave. I see now that all they had to do was look at me to know how serious my cocaine addiction really was, regardless of what I said. My physical appearance was evidence that I was dying of something.

To admit defeat, to say I had failed at so many things was really shameful and painful. I had been powerless all my life, and I was not about to give these strangers power over me too! I fought to hold on to what little power I thought I had. The position they wanted me to take appeared to be weak and out of control. "No!" I shouted. "I can't do this!" I was already feeling shame and guilt about how I had been treating my children and my family; what more did they want?

I was told that I had to surrender to win. Surrender to win, what kind of sense does that make? How can you possibly surrender to win? In my neighborhood, you never surrendered; that was only for the sissies and was not relevant to me.

What I had come to realize was that this type of surrender starts the process of healing. To admit that I have failed helps me find my healing. Surrender did not mean that I am a failure; what it meant was that I had botched up my attempt to be a mother, wife, friend, etc. because of my drug addiction. "Surrender to win" means I don't have to fight my problems, my pain, or my situation alone anymore. What a relief to admit!

In dealing with this paradox of "surrender to win," I am reminded of a time when I was maybe eleven or twelve years old. I grew up as a tomboy, and I fought a lot with my brothers. My older brother, who was physically stronger than me, would hold me down and twist my arm behind my back, and he would say to me, "Surrender." I would say, "No!" He would try to inflict enough pain on me that I would eventually surrender. Well, this went on for quite some time, and I thought it made me strong not to give in. I would hold out as long as I could, and it would force him to surrender instead. My brother would always walk away from me, convinced that I was crazy. Well, I didn't care that he thought I was crazy; not surrendering was my reward. I didn't care about the pain as long as I felt that I had won. I thought I could live with the pain as long as I did not let go or give in, and as long as my brother didn't see me as a loser. I have to confess that I have used this type of destructive thinking in many areas of my life throughout the years, not knowing when to surrender. Growing up with the belief that if I surrender I lose has caused me to lose many valuable things in my life.

As I look back today, I am amazed at the simplicity of surrender. When I took another look at this paradox of "surrender to win," I understood that all I had to do in order to stop the pain was say to my brother, "I surrender!" Who was really the winner at that point? To say the humbling words "I surrender" would have stopped so much unnecessary pain for me. I took some unnecessary beatings in my life because my pride kept me from surrendering.

I had to admit that I needed help. The most important person to admit it to was myself, as I have heard so many times "to thy own self be true." Self-deception is a dangerous thing; it is a prison that we make for ourselves. We become skilled at deceiving ourselves, and it doesn't take a drug to accomplish this task of lying to ourselves. I have lied to make myself look good and feel better. What I failed to realize was that I could not look good all the time.

This first step to healing is similar to the episode with my brother. We surrender to stop the madness in our lives. We surrender to start the healing process. We surrender to that person, place, or thing that is causing our lives to be unmanageable and causing the unnecessary pain by our saying, "I can't handle it." We realize that we have no power over it alone. We need help! Admitting our weakness opens the door for recovery and healing to start.

In my weakness, I am made strong, in view of the fact that the strength I show is not my own. A friend lost to the cocaine addiction went to treatment for help. She stayed sober about thirty days. Consequently, the pull of addiction was too much for her; she came to my door seeking to buy cocaine. Her comment was, "I'm just weak. I can't handle it." Little did she know the power of those words. We are weak, but our strength is in the Lord. Tragically so, she turned her life over to her addiction and cocaine; therefore, the next thing I heard was that she was killed in a drug-related accident, only days later. Today I say, "I'm weak. I can't handle it, but I know someone who can."

CHAPTER TWO
"GOD CAN!"

"The father instantly replied, 'I do believe, but help me not to doubt.'"
(Mark 9:24)

I went from hopeless to hopeful. My addiction had robbed me of my choices and controlled my whole person. It told me when to sleep, when to eat, how to be a mother, not to pay my bills, what to say, how to love, who to love, stand up, sit down, roll over, etc, and I obeyed. I was a puppet in its hands. I was insane, and I needed to be restored to sanity. Well, what happened now was that I needed something other than drugs and all my little gods to fill my emptiness inside.

Addiction becomes a god that we worship daily. Addiction is a thief, and it robs! A friend of mine would say, "Addiction wants us dead, and it will not stop until the job is done." I see it as a "hit-man" following me around, watching, studying me, waiting for the perfect opportunity to take me out, and he is good at what he does. The Bible refers to our enemy as a thief that roams around like a lion, looking for whatever he can steal, kill, or destroy, and that is usually us! When we are in addiction, we are slaves in enemy hands, separated from God, and when we are separated from God, we are lost. I had to come to know that God could help me with my problem. "I can't, but He can." Although we may be saved sometimes, we do not accept or utilize God's power in our lives.

My mind was my enemy, and when left alone with my mind, it put me in bad company. So many times I made decisions that were insane because of my thinking. My focus was on getting my drug, and everything else came second, including feeding my children. I'm not proud of what I've done; it's just true. My thinking was insane; it was not sound. For instance, I recall my rent was $350.00. I managed to come up with $300.00, and my reasoning said, "Well, you don't have all of it so just get high with what you have; don't pay the rent." It made sense to me so I got high with the money.

In the process of my bad decision-making, there was always something inside of me that whispered, "You don't want to do that." The problem with choice is that sometimes our "will" conflicts with God's "will."

My choices have brought me unnecessary pain, addiction, compulsions, difficulties, and self-defeating behaviors, but it is God's plan that will bring me healing. You will hear me say it over and over again in this book, "God says we are to renew our minds." I realized that my mind and my heart were working against each other. The healing process of renewing my mind would bring my heart and mind together working for my good.

My cocaine addiction robbed me of the power to choose; it made my choices for me. Our power to choose is probably the most powerful thing we have, and whatever we give our power over to is what controls us. Where a man's heart is, is where his treasure is. Sometimes that controlling factor can be something very simple, even something that was meant to be good. The apostle Paul talks about being controlled in 1 Corinthians 6:12. He states, "Everything is permissible in this world, but not everything is beneficial." He went on to say, "I will not be mastered (controlled) by anything."

To be mastered by anything other than God Himself makes me insane. I have been told that insanity is repeating the same things over and over and over and over, expecting something different to happen, expecting it to work each time. Insanity is a vicious cycle that keeps going and going. The insanity in my life kept me doing things against my will. One Christmas close to the end of my addiction, I had no money to buy presents for my children. Of course, I had already spent it all on using cocaine and other drugs. So I went to my dope-dealer boyfriend and got a good amount of money for Christmas. The bills were all small bills, so I went to the store to exchange them for larger bills. And I went back to my boyfriend with his money to purchase his cocaine as if I was doing it for someone else. Two days later, I was back asking him for more money. He gave me more money. I couldn't help myself, and I repeated the same thing. I believed that he didn't know what I was up to and the cocaine we had was the best in town, (which in the end were both lies). Now it was Christmas Eve, and I was out of money again with no presents for my children. I humbled myself, or actually humiliated myself, and returned to him again, begging for more money. This time, I ended up with only $200 to spend for three children. Well, as the story goes, I couldn't stop myself. I spent $150 on cocaine and only $50 on my children for Christmas. I can't even begin to tell you what this felt like. In the midst of insanity, I could not stop using cocaine until all the drugs and money were gone, then I would look for rest. I lived the vicious cycle, waking up each day repeating the insanity of smoking cocaine and using other drugs, knowing that it was causing me mental, physical, and spiritual pain. I made vows to myself each day to quit only to let myself down time and time again.

One reason we stay in our insanity is that we believe no one will know what we are doing, because it is done in the dark, in secret. Abuse or sin is done behind closed doors, and we think we can get away with it. We may think, "One more hit, one more time, then I'll quit." But to live this way is to live in insanity. **Psalms 10:10–11,** *"The helpless are overwhelmed and collapse; they fall beneath the strength of the wicked. The wicked say to themselves, 'God isn't watching! He will never notice!'"* What foolish thinking, it always leads to needless problems.

I had many problems beneath my drug addiction, and I didn't know the way out of my insanity. I was tired of covering up and pretending that I had no problem when everyone around me knew that I did. My family told me I had a problem, but all it resulted in was me using more drugs to cover the pain of the shame and guilt of the truth. This problem that I had was bigger than me, so common sense would say I needed something bigger than me to fight it. How insane would it be to go into battle with one man and one gun against an army of five hundred men with five hundred guns? It is an extreme example, but it symbolizes the structure of the way my life was going, always against the odds. My life was unmanageable, and I was powerless to change it. An unmanageable life is an unproductive life.

I had to confront the distorted images I had of God to start my healing. I heard about God, but I didn't really know Him for myself. I did believe my grandmother knew Him. I remember her as a God-fearing, praying, and giving woman. All I knew was that I had tried everything, so why not give God a try? I needed something other than myself because "me" alone was in bad trouble, and my best thinking was insane. I had to make a choice to be free or stay in bondage. Insanity is living in bondage and being held back by forces we cannot see; it's an internal domination. I had so many internal conflicts that I had to come to believe in my heart that God was able and willing to help me. I needed so much to be restored and delivered from my death. I didn't want to be crazy anymore, but my past experiences made me feel unworthy of God's love or His deliverance. I can't let my past keep me from changing. My old life had to die so I could live. Sometimes we have to stop something old in order to start something new. We exchange our old beliefs, ideas, actions, and lifestyles for new ones.

I needed the faith to believe that God would restore me, take care of me, and provide for me. I thought God had turned his back on me so it was difficult to believe in Him. My sweet grandmother, bless her heart, in her desperate attempt, tried to help me get on the right track and do what was right as a young child. She told me that God was a forgiving God, and if I continued to do wrong, He would surely get tired of me. Her tactics

13

are understandable to me today, but back then, they backfired. Instead of me changing my ways, I turned the opposite way and believed God had to be tired of me already. I mean, come on; I had already done many bad things my grandmother knew nothing of, so I decided what's the use? I would continue to do things my way. As a young adult, I realized that the belief that she put in me was still with me. The devil is our enemy, and he wants me to stay hopeless, and God wants me to be hopeful because faith releases our healing. God can change our name from worthless to worthy and put us on the winning side. To be restored to sanity means to go home to the Father and reconcile our relationship with Him. What I needed most was a relationship with God.

I attended a healing service a few years ago and watched people being healed. As I left, I saw this long line of people still sick, crippled, dying, in wheelchairs, and unhealed. I was truly puzzled at why God did not heal them. So I said, "Lord, you are the healing, so why didn't these people get healed?" He said, "They came to see the preacher, and their healing was more important than the 'One' that can heal them." Much like the crowd that surrounded Jesus in His days on earth, most of the people came to see the magic, as they would attend a magician's show. They had no interest in the Master. God says, "Seek ye first the Kingdom of God and all these things will be added unto you." It is through our faith relationship with God that we are made whole.

I once heard a man say, "Faith sees what is happening, but it does not agree with it." We have to take hold of our situations, our lives, and reach out to Jesus for our healing! Faith is about a relationship with the Lord. It is about knowing the "Truth." When we learn the truth, we look past the situation that doesn't line up with God's Truth.

The woman with the issue of blood in the Bible, Luke 8:43–48, had been dealing with an issue for many years and was healed by her faith. The Bible gives accounts of many people who were healed by their faith. We are told that it is faith that moves God. This woman's faith believed if she could just get to Jesus and touch Him, she would be healed from her hurts. When she touched Him, she took hold of the healing power of Jesus because of her faith. Some have said that she put a demand on His ability to heal her, and her faith moved God. She is our example. Oh yes, **"HEALING HURTS,"** but in order to make it, we must keep our eyes and senses on Jesus and not the pain.

This woman in her predicament, crippled by an evil spirit, deliberately set out after Jesus for her healing. Intentionally in the midst of her pain, in the midst of the ridicule and comments from the crowd, she touched Jesus with her faith. She had one thing on her mind: "If I can just get to Jesus!"

This woman allowed nothing to stop her or distract her from getting to her "healing." Sometimes we have to go through many obstacles to find our healing. This woman in Luke chapter eight had a reason, a cause, a situation that forced her to seek the Savior. Her troubles forced her to seek the only "One" that could help her. The truth is that her condition left her with many other issues even after the bleeding stopped. She still had to take care of the business of being rejected by her family and all the people. In addition, she had spent all her money on doctors and don't forget her reputation of being unclean. Her illness had left her stained, and this woman needed to be cleaned. For me as well, once the drugs were out of my life, I was able to see so many other issues in my life that needed healing. I had been crippled by my addiction.

I came to realize that no human power can heal my hurts. No human power can relieve me of my past. God is the only one that can restore me to sanity and deliver me from my past. Like the prodigal son, I had to come to my senses and take a good honest look at **my life** and **myself.** I was living like some type of animal when my Father had a much better life for me. When we are confronted by the truth, we have to make a decision. God accepted me as I was, and what I needed was to be reconciled with Him. I made a decision to return home to the Father and start to live the life He prepared for me.

God wants us to be whole, and this takes healing. The point is that no matter what happens in our lives, our best bet is to turn to God first. I have turned to so many things to fill me up or make me feel good, and they just don't work. Each and every day, I pursued compliments from others, especially men, to make me feel good about myself. I have had several marriages that didn't work. I never understood that I was the daughter of the King and I didn't have to settle for less. (This is the message I give to my children: don't settle.) I had relationships with everything else—men, women, drugs, money, sex, excitement—and no relationship with God the Father. I lacked the most important relationship of all!

Being out of a relationship with God left me totally insane, and restoration was exactly what needed to happen for my sanity to return. The only way to be reconciled with the Father is through Jesus. Jesus reveals the Father, and the Holy Spirit leads us to Jesus. The only way to the Father is through Jesus! He is the truth, the way, and the light! I was out of relationship with God. I was His enemy and unfamiliar to Him and His ways. My healing was tied up in my belief in Jesus and accepting Him as my Lord and Savior. Jesus came into this world that we may be reborn again into freedom. We have to come to believe in God's love for us, which is the greatest power we can have.

When Jesus died on the cross for us, it was an act of God's love. Jesus is God's love fulfilled, made complete. Love meets the need, and I was dying in need of a Savior. God raised Jesus from the dead, and He ascended to Heaven and took a seat on the right-hand side of God, where He is interceding on our behalf. Moreover, before He left this earth, Jesus said He would not leave his people comfortless, so He left his Holy Spirit that lives in the hearts of the believers. Jesus is not a temporary fix! He is not looking for a short-term home in our hearts. He wants to take up permanent residence in our lives. Jesus is not just passing through; He is here to stay!

The bottom line is that we have to know God's love for us. I mean, really believe His love for us, not just as something to say because it is the Christian thing to do. My life really moved to a higher height when I realized His love for me on a deeper level. I realized that not only did I need to go home to the Father but He was there waiting on me. Yet, while I was out there in the world, shaking it up and down on the dance floor, using drugs, lying, stealing, cheating, and being whatever my drug needed me to be, God was waiting on me! And when I came home, He met me with a hug and a kiss after all I had done. As I live and grow closer to God, each step closer brings me into a new excitement and revelation of His wonderful life-changing love and power! While time passes and struggles come, I have to hold on to the unconditional love of His hug and His kiss.

The apostle Paul prayed in the book of Ephesians that we would know the love of Christ, that we may be rooted and grounded in His love, that we would know the **scope** (extent) and **measurement** (capacity) of His love. God's love is so wide and long that it reaches out to the whole world, to people we can't reach, and He will not stop until His Glory can be seen. Every knee shall bow, and every tongue will confess that God is King. His love is so high that it rises all the way to the throne of God through our praise. His love is so deep that it is loaded in knowledge and wisdom. It is so deep that it reaches to the bottom of all our discouragements, hopelessness, and even death; nothing can separate us from His love.

Furthermore, we have a High Priest that can be touched by the feeling of our infirmities; He knows what we feel. Jesus has already experienced our weaknesses, and therefore, He understands us and can help us with our hopelessness. Even when the world shuts me out, I remember that I can never be lost to God's love. It's comforting and reassuring to know that nothing can separate me from His love. We will be more successful if we can make it personal. God so loved me that He gave His only begotten Son. **God is an amazing and awesome love!**

Some of us have been guilty of being confused about love. We think love is a feeling, but love is actually an action that produces a feeling. There are times when love can be very painful. Jesus is our greatest example of love; His dying on the cross says it all. The Bible says the greatest display of love is when we can lay down our life for a friend.

Over the years, I came to know God's love more intimately. God opened my eyes and heart to a deeper revelation of his love through another friend's death. In my addiction, I was surrounded by people who were rejecting God for drugs; as a result, there were many sad stories and horrible endings. Anyway, no one in this world but God and I knew what this friend meant to me or knew the revelation that He gave me after her death. She struggled most of her life with drug addiction until one day it took her life. I felt such a deep sorrow as I wept about her death. The Holy Spirit is the only one that can lead us into the vastness of the love of Christ because it is beyond our comprehension.

The Spirit revealed to me that I was mourning the loss of my friend's love for me not my love for her. She loved me more than I loved her. As it is with Christ, it is about his love for me and knowing His love for me, not my love for him. I knew without a doubt that this woman loved me, and that "knowing" did not come to its exactness until her death. God wants me to "know" that He loves me without a doubt and understand what my life would be like without the love of Christ. I know my friend did not die for me, but her death was used to draw me closer in relationship with God.

The pain in our lives can draw us closer to God or separate us. Most of all, Jesus died for me that I might have a closer relationship with God. He opened the door that had been closed to me for so long, the door to true freedom and healing. The sad thing is that everybody can make it but they don't; some have to die so that others can live. When addiction takes a life, it reminds me how much I need God to stay sober. Some people reject God, and when we reject Him, it puts us in a position to be mastered or destroyed by something else.

Healing can be a process that requires time, patience, and faith—especially during the times we want to quit because the pain and fear are so overwhelming. We are in a war to become whole again. We are in a war that can only be won by fighting to the end! So don't quit! Faith keeps us in the race. Jesus told many that were healed in the Bible, "It was your faith that healed you, saved you, made you whole or changed your life."

This process of life can sometimes be so unbearable that we want to quit and go back to our old ways of coping. Don't quit in the middle of the process; don't quit in the middle of the storm. Most of the time when we want to quit, it is usually in the middle of the storm, never before, at the beginning, or at the end. The middle of the storm is usually the toughest and most painful, because it's typically when we can't see or hear what's really going on around us. If we quit in the middle, we will stand to lose everything we have fought for, cried about, lost sleep over, prayed about, hurt for, or trained and worked so hard for. When the pain becomes or seems unbearable, don't quit! When the fear seems paralyzing, don't quit! When you fall, get up! Take these failures and use them to initiate a commitment to follow Jesus. Through our trials, we can become more determined to make it. It is an opportunity to make our greatest investment, which is in Jesus, where we will receive our greatest returns.

Isaiah 40:31, *"Because they that wait upon the Lord shall renew their strength; they shall mount up with wings of eagles; they shall run and not be weary; and they shall walk, and not faint."* We have amazing benefits if we wait on the Lord. The Lord said we will **mount** up, meaning we will rise up, get up, increase in level, be made stronger, or prosper.

We need the strength of the Lord, because the world is so insane, agree? It is so broken, but we do not have to be a part of the world. We can believe in our hearts and know in our minds that Jesus is the peace in our storm. He is the only one that the wind and the rain of our storms will obey. Jesus is the one that can restore us to some type of sanity. He is the one that can renew our minds. I struggled with so many things in life, so many attacks of the enemy, but Jesus is the only one that can speak to the turbulence in my life and bring tranquility. I had to come to know that the Lord is always with me. I will not be shaken for He is right beside me. He is my refuge and my strength, an ever-present help in the time of trouble. Coming to believe that God is our everything is a process that doesn't happen overnight. I had to take it easy on myself and remember I didn't get this way overnight and my healing probably wouldn't come that way. So "easy does it," but do it!

In the midst of our storms, we have to get to Jesus, no matter what it takes; we have to get to Him first and stay focused on Him, not the storm around us. I have to have faith in the power of Jesus, not in my own ability. The astonishing fact, to me, about Peter walking on water is that he did it in the middle of a storm. In the middle of the pain, we have to get to Jesus. Peter knew that he had to get to Jesus. Remember, as you read about the disciples in the storms, one fact holds true: Jesus was always there; whether He was asleep or walking on water, HE was there! He is in our boat, so we can cross to the other side!

A full confident assurance that He loves me gives me the ability to do all things. It takes faith to press through the messes of this life. It takes

18

faith to stop using drugs and stay stopped. I lived the lifestyle for so long I doubted whether or not God would help me. God says if we have faith the size of a mustard seed, we can move mountains. Mountains represent the obstacles in our lives. The faith is in God's ability to heal us, not our own ability. If we are wavering in our faith, we ask God as the father asked in Mark chapter nine: "Help me not to doubt!" I believe God's response to this desire of seeking is nothing less than a miracle. What other way can God help our doubt besides performing His power in our lives. I prayed every day for God to take away my desire to use drugs, and one day the miracle happened. I suddenly realized that I no longer wanted to use. God will do for us what we can't do for ourselves. Faith keeps us praying in the storm.

Maybe God has made some of us promises that we've not yet seen; we have been waiting and waiting for a while—maybe to get sober; for our marriages to change; for our finances to change; for jobs, cars, homes, or ministries to change; to save our families, our children, etc. It has been going on for so long we may start to wonder or we may start to doubt if it will ever happen for us. Some even quit waiting; some become discouraged and frustrated. But Jesus said in Mark 9:23, "Anything is possible if a person believes." The father of the son in this story spoke in doubt to Jesus, "Do something if you can." Jesus said, "If I can." The problem was not with whether or not Jesus could, it was with "if I can." "If I can" believe nothing is too hard or difficult for God. Faith is not magic, and it's not just positive thinking; it's obedience that comes from a relationship with Jesus.

The most important thing is that Jesus has to be bigger than our problems. He has to be bigger than abuse, fear, sexual abuse, drugs, alcohol, money, adultery, or what you did last night! God is the light at the end of the storm. He is the light in our darkness. The devil wants to keep us in darkness, which keeps us in shame. Our only job is to believe that it is true and stay connected to Him through prayer. Jesus says, "I Am the vine and apart from Me you can do nothing. I Am what you need in the middle of the storm." All we have to do is open the door of our hearts and invite Christ in. The Holy Spirit will guide our steps in everything that we do. Jesus said, *"Here I am! I stand at the door and knock, If anyone hears my voice and opens the door, I will come in and eat (fellowship) with him, and he with me"* **(Rev. 3:20)**. Jesus wants in our hearts to have a relationship with us.

I have truly come to believe more and more that God really loves me, and I have come to know the power that it holds in my life. God has demonstrated His love in my life time and time again. God wants what is best for us. If we trust and wait on God, our faith will grow through experience with Him. He loves me in spite of what I have done in the past. He loved me right into repentance. I had to come to believe by faith that God is my healer, and He can restore me to sanity through Jesus and make me whole. God can carry our load!

"ON CHRIST THE SOLID
ROCK I STAND,
ALL OTHER GROUND,
IS SINKING SAND."

CHAPTER THREE
"HERE, GOD, YOU DRIVE!"

"Then Jesus said, 'Come to me, all of you who are weary and carry heavy burdens, and I will give you rest. Take my yoke upon you. Let me teach you, because I am humble and gentle, and you will find rest for your souls. For my yoke fits perfectly, and the burden I give you is light.'"(Matthew 11:28-30, New Living Bible)

Regretfully, my past held so many hurts and disappointments that I swore to protect myself, and in doing so, I have tried to control every area of my life, and I blocked God out. I was god in my life; I was driving the car. I don't know why the idea of having control was so important to me because it is only an illusion. Who really has control? God is the only one in control; nothing happens in God's world by mistake. Although we have freedom of choice, it doesn't equal control. I had to give up the desire for control and know that **God can!** Meaning God is able. I had to hand over the keys.

I can't catch up with lost time, and I can't live down my past, but God can deliver me from it. My past has proven that I had been living in bondage and that beyond a shadow of a doubt, God is on my side. I was born in 1958 in Prague, Oklahoma, a small town with very few black people. I was related to most of the people in my neighborhood or we all knew each other. Each day that I can remember was embraced with racism or some type of abuse. But in the midst of the pain, there were some good times too. My days growing up in Prague, Oklahoma, I was known as a rebel. When I was old enough to understand what was happening and old enough to fight, I started fighting to survive. It was the only thing I knew to do. I grew up with four brothers who taught me to fight, play football, and climb trees.

I recall as a child around the age of eight believing that God made a mistake with me because I could not figure out a reason for my life. I wondered, "Why did He make me?" I had the belief that I did not fit in this world and I was really different from not only the white people in my town but my friends as well. I thought as a child that God was a racist old white man, who was always looking for me to trip up and do something wrong so that he could check it off on his list of reasons to send this little colored girl to hell! I believed that God wanted nothing to do with me; how could He after allowing me to live in such a mess!

My home was different from my classmates'. In at least three houses I lived in as a child, I remember not having a bathroom on the inside. Our bathroom was an "outhouse," and our bathtub was an old tin tub that we had to pour heated water into in order to bathe. Sometimes we had to do our business in a tin can and carry it to the outhouse. My childhood was surrounded by embarrassment and shame. But there was Mama who was always there, always making a way although we were dirt poor. Many times I wondered, "Where is this God?" If I wasn't fighting the white people in my town because of the ill treatment, I found myself having to fight the men in my neighborhood to keep them off of me.

I tell of my childhood because I felt my drinking and drugging was a direct result of trying to escape the memories. The overall message I received most of my childhood was that I wasn't good enough. So I sought to escape reality at an early age. I was a daydreamer and became pretty good at it. I created my own world in my mind because in my world I could be good enough and what or whoever I wanted to be. I believe this is the reason why I liked drugs so much; they took me away from my reality.

All the pictures I saw of God portrayed Him as a wise old white man, and all the people I saw living a life of success were "white" people. I knew something was wrong with this image. I thought God was playing some cruel joke with us (black people), and how could He be a part of my life? Because of the racism and the drastic imbalance of the races, I believed that God made my life the butt of somebody's joke, and it left me really bitter and angry. As a result of my distorted beliefs, my relationship with God for many years was a love-hate relationship. A part of me feared Him because He was God, but this fear was not one of respect; it was terror. On the other hand, there was a part of me that resented Him because of the things I had to go through.

Trying to shake these old beliefs and habits is really difficult, and it takes time to reprogram our minds. Just when you think you're over it, those thoughts creep right back in without notice. My past experiences, whether "good" or "bad," dictate who I am today, and it can keep me in bondage if I let it. If we don't deal with the issues or ghosts from the past and put them to death now and forever, they will prevent our healing. God wants to heal our scars and hurts from the past.

My life was unmanageable due to my own thinking and my own actions. Subsequently, the thing that had become evident is that during most of my young adult life I had no idea of how to manage my own affairs. I needed a manager; I needed somebody to direct and manage my thinking and my actions. I could no longer do it on my own, and I had to become sick and tired of myself before I could say the words, "God, I am depending on You, or here, God, You drive!" One thing I knew for sure was that my choices up to this point in my life had only led to regret and more regret!

My thinking alone always led me to a dead end. I thank God that in the midst of losing everything because of my drug addiction, I hit bottom, and it forced me to look at what was left: "me"! A choice had to be made: Will I choose life or death? Many times when we hit bottom, there is only one way we can look, and that's up. I had to stop demanding my own way all the time because I just might get it and the consequences that go along with it.

Once God is the director of our lives, our whole lives start to change. This is really a fearful action to take, to allow God to direct and manage my life, especially because I was used to trying to control my own business. Moreover, it is a decision that we have to make for ourselves; nobody can make this choice for us. This resolution put fear in me because I really thought God would have me doing some things that I really did not want to do. I wanted God to take the drugs out of my life, but He was starting to ask a little too much. My imagination ran away with me; I really did not want to go door to door with my Bible, bugging people, or stand outside of the stores trying to put a pamphlet in somebody's hand. Lord knows! I did not want to give up my miniskirts and my makeup. I remember saying, terrified, "What is this 'God' going to have me do? I just can't do it! I can't do this!" I couldn't imagine anyone having that kind of power over me! In actuality, I had been turning my will and life over to destruction.

At that point in my life, my drug addiction had me by the throat, and all I wanted to do was just stop using drugs; I didn't bargain for all this. I had a feeling that God had bigger plans than what I bargained for. You see, I was accustomed to using God as a "bellhop"—someone to run errands for me. I only called on Him when I needed Him and got angry with Him when He didn't show up on my time or when I expected Him to. But you know, God is not my genie in the bottle; He is my Savior, my Lord, my Father, my Provider, and my Healer with His own time.

My addiction had me caught up for so long that I forgot how to live and love. So I needed to be taught; I needed to allow God to do what He does best, to be God in my life. God wants us to live life, and the Bible is our guide on how to live. I had to make a decision to trust God with all my situations, and this does not make me perfect; this was an opportunity to choose. My chance to choose between life and death was standing before me. God was offering me His Grace. God gave me my choice back after drugs had taken it away, and choice is a powerful tool to have. My world was consumed with fear; I was so afraid, afraid to stay where I was in my life and afraid to move on. I was stuck again. I had lived most of my life tormented by fear, especially after years of abuse.

I lived my life afraid to win and afraid to lose based on my past. When I was the age of about twelve or thirteen, I was in a "track meet" for my school. I didn't think I was qualified to be there, but others seemed to think I was, like my coach. Well, the race began, and when I realized that I was winning the race and by a great length (if I may say so!), immediately I felt an overwhelming fear that I was doing something wrong and I did not deserve to win. So I reacted in fear, and I ran off the track in the middle of the race. (The story of my life: I ran off the track in the middle of the race; I ran off the track in the middle of my life.) My coach had this shocked look on his face that I'll never forget as he ran over to me, shouting, "What happened!?" I responded with a lie; I told him that my chest was hurting so badly that I had to quit! I couldn't possibly tell him the truth, that fear was why I quit in the middle of the race. From that point on in my life, I was known for running off the track and quitting the race because of fear. The fear I lived in was the reason drugs and alcohol became a very important part of my life. I thought being high gave me courage, but it only made me quit the race of life. I understand now that to win this race we don't have to run fast; we just have to keep running, and sometimes we may have to slow down the pace to stay in the race. Faith can keep us in the race.

Faith is the opposite of fear, and it takes faith to turn my will and my life over to God. Faith is acting out what you believe, and if we believe we can't make it, we won't. Faith can work for us or against us. It is not just being, and it is not just acting; there is a relationship between faith and work. Sometimes we just have to step into the unknown. The Bible says in Hebrews 11:1 that faith is the confident assurance that what we hope for is going to happen, and it is the evidence of things we cannot yet see. Sometimes we have to just close our eyes and jump! It was by faith the great heroes of faith stepped out; there was always action behind their belief.

My recovery takes me back to many lessons that I learned as a child. My brothers and I were at the swimming pool in our neighborhood, and they conquered the skill of diving. And they were taking turns diving off what we called the "high diving board." I remember wading around in the three-foot pool wishing with all my heart that I could work up enough courage to jump off that high diving board; fear keeps us from operating in faith. I watched them every day, afraid to try it myself. This same fear came over me at a later time in my life when I was faced with taking a leap of faith by making that crucial decision to allow God to manage my life. I knew that this major step would change my life forever. I didn't know if I was ready for the change.

I knew in my heart that if I gave my life to God there was no turning back for me, just like the day I decided to climb up the high diving board and jump! I said to myself, "Okay, this is the day that I jump." I started up the steps of this **monster** diving board, and before I could get to the top, I panicked and made everyone behind me climb down so that I could get off; I changed my mind. Well, I attempted several times to defeat this **dreadful** diving board, but I would always panic with fear.

I still had a desire, so one day I made it to the end of the diving board, and as I turned to look at the people behind me, they were giving me that look of no turning back this time; the only way to go was forward. How many times in my life have the people I have hurt and stepped over because of my addiction gave me that same look? Well, I stood there for a little while on the diving board as my brothers cheered me on from below, and finally I worked up enough nerve to jump with my eyes closed and my hands over my mouth. I jumped from the high diving board!!! When I hit the water, an explosion of excitement came over me. I realized I had done the right thing. I felt like the weight of the world was lifted off my shoulders. I had faced one of my greatest fears at that time in my life. I sprung up out of the water with a shout of victory, and the witnesses were happy for me! Facing our fears is the only way to get over them.

To allow God to manage my thoughts and actions was so similar to this giant leap of faith. I still have a cloud of witnesses to my walk of faith! I still have a shout of victory! I praise God with a shout of victory! The most meaningful insights that I have learned are also the most difficult ones as well. I had to open my mind to God, because my life depended on it.

My decision to allow God to rule in my life is the best decision that I have ever made in my life. I had to make the decision because Jesus is a gentleman. He doesn't kick the door in; He wants us to choose. We have to make a decision to open the door when He knocks, and He is persistent; He keeps knocking until we answer. I am glad that He is a God of second chances and doesn't give up on us. I am a woman who can look at almost every decision I have made in my lifetime and figure out something different I could do to change my life or to improve my choices. Making the decision to get closer to God is the greatest move I could ever make.

At this point in my life, I have tried everything else; why not try God? I had a past that needed to be redeemed and healed. I thank God for my yesterdays and my past for they have been my best teachers.

I desperately desired to be made whole, and I became willing to let God have His way in my life. This decision is based on facts, not emotion. I evaluated the facts and came to the conclusion that I myself am helpless. God's "will" does not always make us feel good although it is always the best way for us. He may even ask us to do some things we don't want to do, but Jesus is our example of doing God's will when it wasn't easy. Jesus said, "Come to me all of you who are weary and carry heavy burden and I will give you rest." Jesus can give us peace for our soul. Peace and serenity will come to us in a way we've never experienced when we allow God to manage our lives. Submission to God's will brings rest for our souls; it brings rest to the torment in our lives.

His Holy Spirit puts us on a path that will lead us to all truth. He directs us away from all addictions, bondage, and sin. With the Holy Spirit working in our lives, we have no room for addiction. I have made a decision to allow God permission to work in my life. If I stay here, then drugs and alcohol have no reason or excuse in my life anymore.

This allows the Lord freedom to be Lord in our lives, the Sovereign Lord in full power, capable of fighting for us and conquering whatever land we need to inherit. Sometimes we want to fight our own battles, but the battle is not ours; it is the Lord's. I do not have the power to fight the disease of addiction because it is too powerful for me alone. But addiction is no match for God, who has all power to drive. Surrendering now gives me the courage to look at myself.

Chapter Four
"The Stuff That's In Us"

"Search me, O God, and know my heart; test me and know my thoughts"
(Ps. 139:23).

Denial is a killer! It closes the window to the "Light." I lied to myself for so long that at one point in my life I could not distinguish the truth anymore. I did not know who I was or where I was going. I had problems, and only through Christ Jesus was God able to heal me. He asked me to show Him who I was, not that He didn't know, but He wanted me to know, and it was done by telling Him. One of the greatest blessings in my recovery is the innermost knowledge of who I am. God wants to remove the core of why I used my addictive behavior to get my needs met. In order to be healed, those things have to be uncovered before the Lord, and then they are no longer underground or hidden. The shame and guilt of my past deeds caused me to cover up.

Secrets keep us sick. One secret sin almost always leads to another. My pastor has said that sin has babies, what an eerie thought! In fact, if I tell a lie, I know I'll have to tell another lie to cover the lie told, and that could really pile up to being a really big mess after a while. The sin just keeps on producing. As we look at ourselves in God's mirror, we see a reflection of who we really are, and we see that our eyes are truly the windows to our souls. God shines His spotlight on us.

With addiction, I had been trapped inside a prison that I made for myself. I worked in a prison setting as a counselor for several years, and the worst prison I have experienced is the one we make for ourselves. I saw people who were behind bars that were actually freer in knowing who they are than many of us who are walking the streets free. We must truly set ourselves free; when we have nothing to hide, we can be released. The difference in the prison we make for ourselves and the prison made for us by man is that we have the key to open the door. So, what is real freedom? Some of us think it is the ability to go where we want or do what we want to do. Real freedom is about knowing who we are in Christ and being able to just be ourselves, as well as functioning in what we know. God is the answer to freedom, and the only way to Him is through His Son Jesus.

When I first took a good look at myself, it was the most painful thing I had ever done. Oh, my God! Is this really me? It couldn't be! I was told,

"Don't fret, Jesus already knows who we are." He even knows our hearts and everything about us. He just wants us to show Him who we are so that He can heal us, and this requires complete honesty on our part. Some of us put on the charade as if we just got it all together even in front of Jesus. We act as if we have no issues, as if we need nothing from God. When we are in His presence, we ask for nothing when we should follow the example of blind Bartimaeus. When he heard the Savior was coming, He began to shout loudly to get His attention. Jesus knew that Bartimaeus was blind, but He still asked him (Mark 10:51), "What do you want me to do for you?" He was saying, "Show me who you are." Does He want to see how badly we really want it? We make an inventory of the stuff that is in us and uncover it before the Lord. He will cover us. Love covers sin. The Good Samaritan, when he saw the man's wounds, the first thing he did was cover them.

I am a woman with issues, and it doesn't mean anything but that I need everything from God. I had to get to a point that I was sick of myself in order to allow God to clean up my life. Most of my problems were a direct result of my own choices. And I thank God that Jesus came into this world for those who are sick, not for those who think that they are well.

In the Bible, Jesus was talking to a peculiar Samaritan woman at the well (John, chapter four). Jesus asked her about a man in her life that He already knew about. She had an opportunity to be honest and do a quick inventory of her life, and she had an opportunity to show Jesus who she was. He knew her past and told her about her future. I found myself like this woman, starving for love and relationships, so much that I made bad choices and welcomed anyone into my life who would have me. Even though there were no serious commitments involved, I accepted what I could get, and I settled for less. Some of us have sought lower companionship to make ourselves feel better about who we really are only to end up in sorrow and pain or wake up in a mess!

This woman from Samaria had issues that caused her to travel alone. Due to the shame and guilt of her issues, I would say she had baggage. In addition, the Samaritan people were known as outcasts, or less than. It is humiliating to be an outcast among people who are considered outcasts. In addition, our issues can cause us to isolate ourselves. Who we are, what we have done, what we think about, what we have not done, what others think about us, and who we are not—all these things are reasons we use that can keep us from the Savior and keep us from knowing who we are. Freedom eludes us. Hear me; if we don't know who made us, how can we know truly who we are? I am a believer that if we don't know where we come from, we surely won't know where we are going and may be doomed to return to our past destructive behaviors. We are required to stand before the Lord naked and let Him point out our flaws. He shines His spotlight on the truth. When God shines His spotlight on us, there is nowhere to hide.

When we are in the presence of God, we cannot help but see ourselves clearly. During this inventory, I found out so many things about myself. God is the only one who can clean us up and heal our hearts. As soon as we see who we are in the presence of the Lord, it breaks us to a point that prepares us for a cleansing. In the presence of the Almighty God, we automatically see our own imperfections.

When we come to the acknowledgement of who we are, the benefits of God await us. We have the information, but until we internalize the information, it does not become real, manifested, or fulfilled in our lives. As soon as we gain the ability to understand who we are in Christ, we become able to face the very thing that had us hiding in our addictions and old destructive behaviors in the first place.

I came to realize that I am the daughter of the King, not just a drug addict, but I have been adopted into the Royal Family, and I am a first-class citizen in the Kingdom of God. Not because I have done some great thing, it is only because of His Grace; He gave me something I didn't deserve. This knowledge allowed me the courage and faith to write this book and share with you God's healing power in my life. I know I was once alien to God and His ways, but the hour has come that I have been brought near to God, by the shedding of the righteous, perfect, and sinless blood of Christ Jesus. Now being His daughter, I can enter into my Father's presence anytime I want to!

God shows us who we are; our only job is to say, "Yes, Lord." There were so many things buried inside, deep within that I thought I would take to my grave. God said to me, "Be free; none of these things are bigger than Me." He gave me the courage to inventory myself, look at my past, abuse, lies, rape, sexual abuse, divorce, relationships, losses, failures, and resentments, so that I may be healed. Through my inventory, I was able to see that I had been foolish, disobedient, silly, stupid, deceived, and enslaved to all kinds of passions and pleasures. I lacked judgment and the common sense it took to just function in this world as God intended. At one point, I would rather smoke cocaine than pay my rent or feed my children. I flirted with death on many occasions, and I was caught up in a whirlwind I couldn't stop on my own.

I had fallen so far down at one point in my drug addiction, I was in a hotel room after hours of smoking crack cocaine, and I knew I had done too much. I was not able to breathe; I could not feel my arms or hands;

my heart felt like it was going to explode inside of me; and the degrading, demoralizing thing is that I begged for one more hit of cocaine. I thought that with the assistance from the person I was getting high with, I could take one more hit from the pipe. I thought that if he would hold the pipe to my mouth, I could manage to take one more breath, one more hit. I was dying for a hit! I was unable to stop myself. This drug owned me! It was my master! As Paul describes in Romans chapter 7: *"I don't understand myself at all, for I really want to do what is right, but I don't do it. Instead, I do the very thing I hate. But I can't help myself, because it is inside of me, this thing inside of me that makes me do these evil things. No matter which way I turn, I can't make myself do right. I want to, but I can't. Oh, what a miserable person I am!"*

I had no discipline in my life. I wanted what I wanted when I wanted it. I was destroying relationships, and I didn't care; the drugs had me numb. My life was full of hatred, anger, and conflict. I caused pain and hurt to many people that got in my way. I lived a life of discontent, always wanting something I couldn't have. I carried my negative feelings in my heart throughout my life, and that kept me in bondage. I carried secrets, memories, guilt, losses, failure, adultery, lost dreams, poverty, a broken heart, and broken relationships like a bag lady. I kept them tucked neatly away. Until God said, "Show me your mess that you may be healed." I had to show him all the mess! It's similar to being caught shoplifting; you have to bring out each individual item to be seen and accounted for. And God shines His spotlight on each and every item found.

I had been yoked together with my past, and I didn't leave home without it. When we are yoked together with something, it means we are on common ground, moving on the same course, and we have the same focus. **Point to ponder: If you're yoked with addiction, you're headed toward death!** So many of us have been unable to move freely with God because we are yoked together with our past or with the pain of our past or some destructive behavior. God wants us to be free, and there is freedom in Jesus.

We have to uncover and face our insanity before God so He can heal us, pull us out of our pain, and put us back together. When the woman with the issue of blood from the Bible (in Mark chapter 5) sought healing in the hem of Jesus' garment, she uncovered herself before Him, and in her faith, she told Him the whole story of what she had been through, and she was healed, set free, and made whole!

Looking at these areas of my life was extremely painful, but in order to heal my brokenness, I had to take a deep look and remember that God is always with me. I had to face my brokenness in order to let it go. God is awesome, and He has the power to <u>call</u> us out of the misery left from past sins. God's words are so powerful that all He had to do to create this world was speak. He sent His Word to heal us. Jesus called Lazarus out from the dead with His words. Even death has to obey our LORD. He is a God who doesn't perform funerals, but He speaks life to the dead. If Jesus can call Lazarus out from death, He can call us out of our mess or the mess we've made of our lives. God wants us to turn everything over to Him, and that includes our will and our lives, the way we think and what we do.

God can call us out of our dead situations just like He did with Lazarus. Jesus called Lazarus from the dead as He did several others. When all hope was gone, Jesus demonstrated the love and power of God by speaking life into dead situations. He was able to display His power over death, and God got all the glory. Whatever your situation, Jesus is saying to us today, He can call us out of it. He will call you by your name. There is no situation too big for God. If we give to God all our stuff and repent, He has the power to call us back from the grief we hold on to. I often wonder where I would be without the Mercy and Grace of God. It brings tears to my eyes, sadness and fear to my heart to imagine the life I would continue to live without God. Living in this world without God is the walking dead!

When we see ourselves for who we really are, we have a tendency to want to hide. We feel a need to not only cover up the outside but the inside as well. Most of the time, the things we are hiding on the inside are what we try to cover up on the outside. It is easier to cover up the outside than to deal with what's on the inside, because HEALING HURTS. We can only be cleansed from the stains of our past from the inside out. Many Christians are delivered, but they are not free!! When we see pain coming, we step out of its way and try to avoid it. "I cannot clear up my past if I cannot face it."

The stuff in us can hold us back from being blessed, and we need to get rid of all the unfruitful things in our lives that are taking up space. What stuff are you made of? We have to search ourselves, as we would clean an old storage room. Look through all the dust and separate the things we need to keep from the things we need to throw away. Some things can be cleaned up, polished, and used again, and some stuff has to go, and we won't know until we do the inventory.

The healing process from addiction includes a personal inventory, and by doing this inventory on myself, I discovered that there were things in me that were not right, things that hurt me and caused pain for others too. I was aware that I covered up a lot of anger that I didn't know how to express, and God is the only one who can hear my anger without being offended. I needed God to search my heart and help me with my inventory. As a result of my past life, I had become very angry. I believe I was angry at the world and felt that the world owed me something. I wasted a great deal of time making others pay for my losses, slack, brokenness, and pain. In addition, I used my anger to protect myself from being harmed again or letting anyone get too close. I found fear was hiding behind my anger. I was afraid of so many things and not willing to admit it, and facing my past was the greatest fear. I had the belief that if I looked back, it would hurt too much. Today a good feeling comes over me to know that God understands our emotions and feelings because He gave them to us.

In the Bible, Jeremiah, Job, and David were men of passionate feelings. One thing they had in common was that they were truly honest with God about how they felt. We can learn from them; they didn't try to be something they were not, no matter how it looked. Jeremiah is known as the "Weeping Prophet" because he cried for his people, but most of all, he felt feelings of hurt, anger, discouragement, fear, depression, and loneliness, which are some of the same feelings we feel. Furthermore, God accepted Jeremiah's emotions, so we should be free to bring all our true feelings to God too, no matter what they are, because He really does love us and He is ready to heal us.

If we are saved and not free to be who we are, could it be our past and hidden secrets holding us back? Could it be satan using these things against us to keep us in bondage? I was a mess undone, and I needed to find the hurt so it could be healed. So many times we are good at pointing out defects that others have and we can't see our own. Why do we try to get the speck out of our brother's eye when we have this 2' by 4" board hanging out of our own? What is the stuff that is in us? What keeps us in bondage? Both are questions we need to ask ourselves. Our healing will make us more equipped to help others.

As I inventory myself, I see that my hurts cut deep and go back as far as 1962, the year my father died; I was only three and a half years old. I was told my father was an alcoholic and that was the reason for his death. He was given poisoned whiskey that killed him, and he was robbed of his money; at the same time, I was robbed of a relationship with my father. The disease of alcoholism took my father! And I have declared war against this enemy! I refuse to go the same way.

As a result of my father's death, I felt abandoned by him. This heartbreaking loss in my life set a pattern that I was not able to see until much later. It clearly had an effect on my choice of men. The preference of men in my life was always the ones who lived on the edge, men who had a difficult time with commitment and stability. This was not a conscious decision on my part most of the time, but subconsciously I knew that they wouldn't stay with me, and the insanity is that's why I picked them. My fear of abandonment caused me to feel insecure and rejected in my relationships and to worry excessively, although my goal was to avoid being alone. In the process of avoiding abandonment, I would sabotage many relationships and run good people away from me to prove that I was right. (I knew they wouldn't stay.) I always sent out double messages that said "come here" and "go away" at the same time. I really hated myself, and it affected my ability to set or achieve positive goals in life. Today, I no longer blame others; I have to accept responsibility for my actions.

We go to God real and honest, and show ourselves to Him. In doing this, we can stop fooling ourselves because God is omnipotent; He sees all and knows all, so we stop wasting time and delaying our healing. We all have something to bring before the Master, no matter what we know, what we have, or what we don't have; we all fall short (Romans 3:23).

I was asked to write about my past as a part of my healing process, and it was an important step to get this stuff out of me. By writing or putting my feelings on paper, it became real. I could no longer manipulate the past; I had to see it for what it really was. As long as the painful memories all stayed in my mind, I could change it, twist it, and make it what I wanted it to be. Most important, it gave the devil something to play with. My denial gave the devil the opportunity and ammunition to fight me with. He constantly whispered fear in my ear, and I was no match for him. Today, I don't have to fight my own battles anymore; the battle is not mine. It is time to come clean! What do we do with our inventory? We give it to God because He is now our manager. If I don't deal with my past, it will come back to haunt me. God can clean up the stuff we found!

CHAPTER FIVE
"COME CLEAN"

"But if we confess our sins to Him, He is faithful and just to forgive us and to cleanse us from every wrong" **(1 John 1:9).**

Confession weakens satan's hold, and confession is powerful because I don't have to carry the burden anymore. We have to come clean with God by confessing our sins verbally one to another that we may be healed. If we give to God all our stuff and **repent**, He gives us a new life, cleansed from our past hurts and armed to withstand any further hurts. When we **repent**, we admit that we have been wrong and make a decision to do right. The action of repentance is to turn away from what's wrong and take the path of God. It is similar to making a 180-degree turn from our old life to the opposite direction, God. I have heard many say that they have made a "360-degree" turn in their lives. If you have, you are still going in the same direction. We must turn from our way to God's way. A 180-degree turn means we turn our backs to the wrong.

God is concerned about the "whole man." He can rebuild our broken lives and give us spiritual prosperity, which never dies. God wants the whole man to prosper. He wants all of me, but there are times I want to bargain with Him and say, "You can have my financial situation but don't mess with my sex life right now." Well, half-measures get us nowhere; we gain nothing; God wants it all! We stop bargaining with Him and become willing to give it all. Destruction comes when we argue against God's way of doing things.

We do have a choice, and our choices can lead us to poverty or prosperity. The Word of God says, "Beloved, I wish above all things that thou mayest prosper and be in good health, even as thy soul prospereth" (3 John, verse two). God offers us a balance in our lives. He is able to restore our losses, take away our shame, and restore the emptiness in our hearts if we allow Him. He is a God that forgives all our sins and is able to heal all of our diseases. God is our Redeemer. **Isaiah 54:4–6a:** *"Fear not; you will no longer live in shame. The shame of your youth and the sorrows of widowhood will be remembered no more, for your Creator will be your husband. The Lord almighty is his name! He is your Redeemer, the Holy One of Israel, the God of all the earth. For the Lord has called you back from your grief."*

When my past was hidden in the dark, the devil had power over me. He used my secrets against me, always blackmailing me into sin. I allowed him to create doubt and fear in my mind. He would say to me, "What would people say if they knew certain things about you?" This would always cause me to hide more and cover up more. The devil loses his power when we can come clean, when we can confess and expose him to the Light; he is no match for our God.

On this journey, we all need a person in our lives whom we can let down with, someone we can take the risk of allowing him or her to see us—in other words, someone who is able to see the good and the bad in us and still love us. It is wise to seek Godly counsel, someone we can tell our hidden ways to, and that person will help us give it to God. Pain shared is pain lessened. Oh, yeah, it's taking a risk, but it is a risk that had to happen for me in order to be healed, because I needed humility in my life. When we confess who we really are to another human being, we develop the character of humility that we need to become a "whole" person. It is important to confess our sins one to another, but we are to be careful whom we pick to confess to, due to the fact that everyone does not have your best interest at heart! Jesus does! Use wisdom! I have started the journey of knowing who I am.

I needed to know who I was and where I fit in; I had no identity. Jesus did not have an identity crisis; He knew who He was and what His purpose on earth was. Well, God wants us to know who we are and our purpose. The way to get started is through healing our hurts, and that hurts! Jesus is the only one I found who can take away my shame, guilt, and loneliness. He alone can comfort me. As I started to see the stains in my life, I started praying more, and I started seeking God's Word more. **Psalms 19:12,** *"How can I know all the sins lurking in my heart? Cleanse me from these hidden faults."* I can't know unless God shows me.

God can wash all the stains of our sin and break the bondage that keeps us in slavery. Then we will know ourselves better and walk the talk, as well as walk in the gift God has given us that was smothered by so much stuff and mess. Some of us talk better than we walk, and some are walking and not talking, but when we are made whole, our **talk** will line up with our **walk.**

Self-awareness is one of my greatest gifts from God as a result of being healed. To live unaware of who we are and God's Mercy and Grace is lethal; it's deadly. I can tell you that through most of my life I was unaware that God was protecting me. As I look back at how far I have come, I know it was His protection, because my thinking was distorted and my mind needed to be renewed. Daily I flirted with death.

When I was high on alcohol or drugs, I could imagine most anything, and in my mind, I could be anybody I could conjure up depending on my mood and hairstyle. In reality, I didn't have to conjure up false images; we all have a gold mine hidden inside of our lives that's just waiting for us to start the dig and search to find it. I don't have to pretend that I am somebody, because I am somebody, in Christ! As we press toward the mark of the High Calling, we aim high and we dig deep. We put forth the effort; it will not just happen! I desire much better than what I have allowed myself to have.

Thankfully, when I open up my past to God by confessing my wrongs to Him, to myself, and another human being, He was able to shine light on a dark situation. The power of our secrets are weakened and removed when exposed to the "Light." Our secrets grow in the dark, and the devil knows this fact; that is why he wants us to keep secrets, but darkness is no match for the "Light." Only until we confess our sins and bring them out into the open can we be free of the destructive cycles in our lives. Self-disclosure is a risk, but it is one we must take.

Sin must be confessed. In **Psalms 32:5,** the Word says, *"Finally, I confessed all my sins to you and stopped trying to hide them. I said to myself, 'I will confess my rebellion to the Lord.' And you forgave me! All my guilt is gone"* (New Living Translation). I believe God is just waiting to heal us, but we tie His hands with unconfessed sins. *"People who cover over their sins will not prosper. But if they confess and forsake them, they will receive mercy"* **(Prov. 28:13; New Living Translation).**

In order to become whole in this process of healing, we need humility, acceptance, and forgiveness. When I confess my sins to another person, humility is developed in my character. When I confess to God, He forgives my sins. God has forgiven me of all my sins through Jesus and my confession. I am made whole through peace and dealing with the characteristics of the way I think, behave, and react. My goal in life is to live in peace with God, myself, and other people. When I confess to myself who I am and what I have done, it is for my acceptance. I have to see the real picture, the whole picture, not just part of it. For the first time in my life, I was introduced to myself. God revealed "me to me" by way of the Holy Spirit. Oh, what a day, because what I found is that I am not as good as I thought I was in some areas and not as bad as I thought I was in other areas, and I had to accept that fact and deal with it!

To come clean is to confess who I am! What will people think? My pastor said that if we do not choose to become humble, life itself will humble us. God says that if we cover our sins we will not prosper; we deny his great promise. Situations, choices, and failures that come up can keep us humble. Our hidden sins can make us live in shame and become so humiliated that we are too embarrassed to face our Lord.

As the woman of Samaria had her conversation with Jesus, she too was introduced to herself. Jesus told her things about herself that were hidden. Sometimes we may know things about ourselves but keep them buried deep inside, sometimes so deep we can't see them. We can cover up with makeup, pretty clothes, nice cars, suits, jobs, professions, education, and all the right words. I had become skillful at dressing up the pain by any means necessary. All our things and baggage can keep us from the Savior and from being healed on the inside. The moment Jesus revealed Himself to the Samaritan woman by letting her know that He was everything she needed, Jesus became what she needed to fill her void. The woman dropped her issues and her past to start a new life and didn't bother to carry it back with her. Addiction is always trying to pull me back in; if I'm not careful, it will succeed.

God rebuilds our broken lives and heals our hurts. Confession of our sins holds a great deal of freedom for us. Most times, there has to be a tearing down before there is a rebuilding. There has to be a death before there is a resurrection, and when we uncover ourselves, God will cover us.

Jeremiah 18:1–4 says, *"The Lord gave another message to Jeremiah. He said, 'Go down to the shop where clay pots and jars are made. I will speak to you while you are there.' So I did as he told me and found the potter working at his wheel. <u>But the jar he was making did not turn out as he had hoped, so the potter squashed the jar into a lump of clay and started again.</u>"* Sometimes when our lives feel like a lump of clay, we are in a prime position for restoration through Christ. As long as I stay in God's hands, there is hope for me, seeing as the potter continues to work with the clay, keeping it soft and workable. It is only when the clay jar or pot hardens wrongly that it has to be destroyed.

In the Potter's hand there is healing; although it's painful, it's healing. I, much like the jar that Jeremiah talks about, did not turn out the way the Father had hoped for me, so I had to be squashed and started over again. I am so grateful that He didn't design me to die a drug addict. I thank God that in spite of everything I am in his hands, in a position to be squashed in the Potter's hands, only to be made better.

God is a refining fire. **Isaiah 48:10**, *"I have refined you but not in the way silver is refined. Rather, I have refined you in the furnace of suffering."* He takes us through the process to be healed, much like the purifying process of gold. The impurities in the gold have to come to the surface in order to be removed. And this is done by turning up the heat or turning up the fire. Sometimes God allows the heat to be turned up in our lives so that He will get the glory, and sometimes that extra heat can be very painful, but it is necessary. Our sufferings in life can be used to refine us, to remove our defects of character. The heat/pain brings the trash to the top so it can be swooped away or removed, and this process continues until the gold is pure and shiny without blemish. This process continues until we come clean and our character shines more like Jesus.

CHAPTER SIX
"LETTING GO OF A LIFESTYLE"

"I know, Lord, that a person's life is not his own. No one is able to plan his own course" **(Jeremiah 10:23)**

The apostle Paul says to strip off every weight that so easily besets us (that is anything that can get in our way of being all that God wants us to be). Paul said his goal was to know Christ more, to be like Christ, and to be all Christ had in mind for him to be. As Christians, we should have the same goal. Forgetting the past is letting it go and not allowing the past to dictate our lives in a negative way. I must lay aside every harmful thing and destructive behavior that is getting in my way. Forsake it, disown it, leaving behind anything that may distract me or hold me back! We become more determined to win this race of life by becoming willing to leave some things behind and allowing God to remove them. For me, I had to let go of a lifestyle, and letting go of a lifestyle that we have grown used to is not easy. Sometimes our first cop-out is to say, "It's too hard." Well, it is hard, but it's not impossible, because we can do all things through Christ who strengthens us. My job is to become willing to get rid of this stuff that continues to get in my way. Changing the way I think and the way I act is letting go of a lifestyle.

I was tired of making the same choices and mistakes over and over again. I really had to become sick and tired of being sick and tired before anything would change for me. Just being aware of my condition and admitting the need for healing did not do the job. Recognizing the need for change and being willing to change are two different matters. We become doers of the Word, not just hearers. Most times, what we do can change how we think, as well as what we think can change what we do.

The process of healing is also a process of renewing the mind. We are as healthy as the choices we make for ourselves. Each person has some type of defect in his or her character that has to be removed. It is a stain left over from the past, or sin. This stain is one you just can't seem to remove or make go away, because only God can remove it. The stains have to be removed because they do not go away on their own. I have been guilty of ignoring my problems, hoping they would lose their power and go away. I survived so long on my defects of character, believing that I needed them for survival. As God started His work on me, removing what

I don't need, I started to grieve the loss, just as I would the loss of someone special; the truth is that my defects were special to me. My feelings were real, my defects were real, and they have been just as much a part of me as my assets, only I used and depended on them more.

I was stuck in a lifestyle, living and believing in my own way. I have wasted time that I can never get back, and now that makes time precious to me. I know I have tried everything else; now it's "time" to try the best. I am at a stage in my life that I am totally ready to allow God to operate in my life fully, even though I still fall short, I still miss it, and I make mistakes. I regret the thought of wasting another moment. My nature has been self-destructive, self-reliant, and defiant. It was my way or no way, and I still have to keep close watch on myself in this area. My old survival techniques do not work, and I had to become willing and ready to let God remove them. They were only temporary fixes that served their purpose only for the moment; my pain would always return.

It was pain that drove me to seek help for my addiction. I wasn't out of drugs or ways to get drugs; it was the **pain** of using that forced me to pursue other alternatives. It had become too painful to use drugs any longer. Pain can increase our desire for change. Although we don't have to always arrive to a state of pain in order to make a decision to change, it is surely a motivating factor. Totally depending on God does not come over night; each level we move to with God brings about a new trust in Him. In my Godly wisdom, I know to trust God, but in my ignorance, I forget and sometimes try to make it on my own. As a result, I need to be reminded that when we fall down we can always get up with God's help. What a love, when each day is filled with new grace and mercy to cover our mistakes. What a mighty God we serve! Each day I wake up, I have another chance to make things right in my life.

I had to commit my healing to God and ask him to take all of me and guide me in my recovery process and show me how to live. God is able to lead us out of any situation that we find ourselves in. I gave up the drugs over sixteen years ago, but I was still living according to the world and my thinking. I was in a relationship with a dope dealer that had instilled fear in my heart. I was afraid to leave him, and I was helping him sell cocaine. I had a hard time giving up this lifestyle. It brought with it benefits and miseries. The money was fast and good, but the heartaches came just as strong and frequent. After being sober for about one year, I started to get a glimpse of what it meant to be free; I was so excited! I started to reflect on how long I had been free. As I thought about who actually made me free and where my freedom came from, I realized that freedom had always been available to me, but I was not aware. Jesus had died over two thousand years ago that I might be free. Oh, my God! What a revelation! All I had to do was choose to be free!

As a black woman, I had looked for freedom in so many things outside of God and outside of myself. I even directed my efforts toward the white people in this world to free me. The Spirit of God said to me, "How can they give you freedom when they don't have it to give? You are waiting and looking for freedom in the wrong places." I was expecting them to give me something that they didn't have because it wasn't theirs to give.

Once God took away the desire to use drugs and alcohol, I had to become willing to let go of a lifestyle, no matter what the consequences were to truly be free. As God delivered the children of Israel from slavery, His next job was to deliver the slavery out of them, which was to change their slavery thinking. God gives us the power to make the change; we just have to be willing.

God had to become bigger than this dope dealer that I feared in order for me to make the change. When I became willing, God made this man as gentle as a kitten to allow me to walk out the door without any type of repercussion. All I know is that I was willing, willing to sacrifice everything for a better way of life, and my life began to change. The things we hold back from God, the things we bargain with, are usually the things we lose. We have to give it up! Every time we become entirely ready for change, things happen!

Our flesh does not die without a good fight. Sometimes it appears safer to go back to what is familiar than to change for the better because the unknown is fearful. I have said several times, "Oh, yes, I let go of that," only to find myself involved again. We can live in a situation so long we become accustomed to it. Some hit bottom and live there with no hopes of ever getting out. I lived in an apartment for several years, and I had this mattress that had a slump in it, and in that slump was a mattress spring that would stick me if I didn't lay right. I learned how to lay just right to prevent it from happening. Many times in our lives, we learn how to adjust to abuse and lack of getting our needs met, not that we like it, we get used to it, because we have done it for so long.

When I finally decided to move into a new place, I had a new mattress with no slump or spring to avoid. I immediately thought, "This doesn't feel right." It wasn't familiar; it didn't feel like mine. I had feelings of wanting to go back to my old place and my old bed because I was familiar with it and knew how to operate. I didn't go back, but the feelings were strong. Many times, I sabotaged good things in my life because I didn't feel worthy, and I needed chaos to feel normal.

41

God's favor helps us to come out of the mess that we can make in our lives and stay out. Being in God's favor is the best place to be. He can cause things to move around and put us in positions we know we don't deserve. The favor of God is so good it feels uncomfortable, but God said to me, "Get used to it; it is the only way for you to come out of your mess." God's favor is the only way to come out of debt and be successful. In this way, with His grace, all will know that it had to be God; I can't for any reason take any glory of my own.

When we obey God, He starts to live in our lives and we put our old lives behind us. *"Do not let any part of your body become a tool of wickedness, to be used for sinning. Instead, give yourselves completely to God since you have been given new life. And use your whole body as a tool to do what is right for the glory of God. Sin is no longer your master, for you are no longer subject to the law, which enslaves you to sin. Instead, you are free by God's grace"* **(Rom. 6:12–14)**. We give ourselves to God knowing that obedience is better than sacrifice. We start to let go of the world and the things in it and start the process of renewing our minds, knowing that this new life God has for us is better than we can imagine. He is able to do far above anything I can ask or think.

It has been a difficult task to grow to the point of willingness to give up my old lifestyle of control and excitement. One idea of fun was going out to the nightclubs. I enjoyed the excitement and attention the nightclubs provided me; I thought at least here I was accepted. The truth is that the devil always had some type of catch for me, waiting to trip me up because of my addiction to excitement. This attraction to excitement has been with me for a long time. As a young girl, I would watch two types of women in my neighborhood: the ones who attended church and the ones who went to the "juke joint" next door to my house. It appeared to me that the women at the club were happier than the women going to church, and they were much younger and prettier too. The women headed toward the church were the older women, and they didn't look too happy. The women at the "joint" had an attraction; they were always laughing with their flashy clothes, cigarettes, and wine glasses in their hands. Something inside of me said, "I can't wait to be like that." I set a goal to be one of those women I saw at the "joint" that appeared to be so happy and alive!

When I became old enough, I fulfilled that goal. I became one of those women I saw at the club, and I found out what was behind the wine, laughter, and flashy clothes. It wasn't as pretty as it looked, and it was deceiving! Consequently, my whole life was centered on this lifestyle of flashy clothes and nightclubs that eventually led to even more drug and alcohol use and promiscuous relationships. I had become captivated to a standard of living that is not pleasing to God.

God is concerned very much about our lifestyle. Pastor Wilma says, "We have a God that gets in our personal business." He wants us to live a life pleasing to live in the Kingdom of God. He asks me, as He is asking you, as He asked the lame man in John 5:5, "Would you like to get well?" The choice is up to us.

When I put my life in God's hands, He started to shape me to fit His purpose for me. We all have a purpose, and only God knows our predestined paths. God is not finished with me yet, and just like the jar in the potter's hands, sometimes we are broken down in order to be made over again. I can say I am being made over into one of God's masterpieces.

My life with Christ is more exciting than the lifestyle I lived. My worst day with Christ is much better than my best day using drugs or being part of the lifestyle I let go.

CHAPTER SEVEN
"THE STAIN REMOVER"

"Oh, what joy for those whose rebellion is forgiven, whose sin is put out of sight! Yes, what joy for those whose record the Lord has cleared of sin, whose lives are lived in complete honesty!" **(Psalms 32:1–2; NL)**

Sin leaves stains and scars in our lives and on our bodies. I have stains left in my life from the sins I have committed, and only God, the Stain Remover, can remove the stains. Even after forgiveness, my past left me crippled and blemished. I am so glad that God does not throw us away when we are soiled, as we do with certain garments that are ruined by stains. Just like a good Father, He was waiting there with His arms open to welcome me back home as I started my way back home. Many times because of my blemished past, I felt unworthy of being healed and unworthy of His love and His welcome. Praise God, there is no stain too tough for Him. He is not shocked by what we do. We can never be too sick for Jesus. **Luke 5:30–32:** *"But the Pharisees and their teachers of religious law complained bitterly to Jesus' disciples, 'Why do you eat and drink with such scum?' Jesus answered them, 'Healthy people don't need a doctor—sick people do. I have come to call sinners to turn from their sins, not to spend my time with those who <u>think</u> they are already good enough.'"* The sicker we are, the more His glory can be seen!

The healing process can be a long process. We can limit God's ability to work in our lives by believing He can only move and operate in certain ways. Humility is extremely necessary when approaching the Holy God. He is a sovereign and omnipotent God. He can move quickly, or He can move slowly, but He is for sure always on time, and that is not our time. God has His own rhythm, and our job is to learn to keep up with it. God is able to talk to us through anything, anyone, and any situation, if we are willing and humble enough to hear him. Which reminds me of a story that reveals His rhythm …

There was a bandleader who had a purpose. He wanted to direct an all-women's band for a special event, different from the all-male band that He usually directed. The bandleader had a rhythm to a song that he tried to teach the women, but every time he tried to teach them the correct rhythm, they responded with the tune of their own rhythm, which was always the same and a lot slower than his. He tried over and over to teach them his rhythm. They knew the song and the words; they just didn't have the right beat, so they could not keep up with the director. So when it was all said and done, the show had to go on, and His purpose had to be fulfilled to have an all-female band. Unfortunately, the women could not pick up the rhythm of the song. So the bandleader had to get rid of the women to accomplish his purpose because they couldn't learn the rhythm. So he had an idea to get his original all-male band and dress them up like women to fulfill the purpose of the women's band that was needed. A funny story, but the moral is God has a purpose that will be satisfied. He has timing and a beat for our lives and this world. In **2 Peter 3:8**, the Word says, *"With the Lord a day is like a thousand years, and a thousand years are like a day."* God's time is not our time. His thoughts are not our thoughts, and His ways are not our ways.

God has a rhythm and a purpose. If we choose not to learn His rhythm and plan, He always has someone else waiting in line. My personal opinion sometimes is that I feel God needs to slow down, and sometimes I feel he needs to speed up, but the bottom line is that I need to keep up and God doesn't need my help.

God has given us basic instructions on how to love and live through His Word, but sometimes we want to play our own song and do it our way! The scriptures hold the truth and mysteries of God and His purpose. The Bible possesses wonderful testimonies of faith walks of men and women to offer us help to continue our faith journey. In the Bible, we find food that feeds our spirit while we are on this spiritual journey to greater faith. In addition, the Word gives insight on truth, faith, grace, sin, salvation, restoration, sanctification, eternal life, and love. Everything we need to clean our lives is there, at the feet of Jesus.

I cannot remove my own defects of character. I have to give up control because when I am controlling, it means I don't need God. When we rest in Jesus, He will clean us up and manifest our gifts. I had to ask God to clean me up, because He is faithful and just and will forgive my sins and "purify me from all unrighteousness" (1 John 1:9). God helps us to see the defects in our characters that need to die. We are sentenced to death, to die a death of our fleshly desires. (HEALING HURTS). If the Holy Spirit does not destroy our defects of character, our defects of character will destroy us. The destruction can come in ways that keep us in bondage and wandering around in the desert for forty years like the children of Israel. We wander around in our own prisons of addiction, fornication, or just sin, not able to make it to our promised land. No one can keep me from my promised land but me.

God took my past experiences, pain, and hurts that I thought were so filthy and washed them as white as snow. Those things that kept me locked down, the things that satan kept using against me, things I carried around like a bag lady—God washed them clean. He took my shameful sexual abuse, rape, addiction, lies, adultery, etc. and all the things that go with that, and He washed it for me. He washed my stains and gave me a new heart. He washed the filthy rags I had in my bag, and He gave me a new bag. The rags in my bag represented my issues. Jesus said, "Take on my yoke for my burdens are light." I no longer have to hide in shame about anything.

God is concerned about my heart. He is concerned about the qualities that we operate out of, which is our character; therefore, He has to clean us up. We don't want to just relax at the point of salvation because there is so much more to life. God does not want us to miss His rhythm. We work out our salvation (Phil. 2:12), and we get better day by day. It's not enough to be saved if we are not going to take advantage of the benefits.

When God cleans us up, it is for His purpose, so His glory can be seen in our lives. God cleans the inside of the cup, and we are restored to a condition of usefulness. Matthew 23:26: *"First clean the inside of the cup and dish, and then the outside also will be clean."* Jesus washes our insides, and then what is on the inside can be seen on the outside. When the cup is cleaned on the inside, then the cup can be used for its intended purpose. A dirty cup on the inside can only be used to fix your eyes on; unless the inside is clean, it can only sit on the shelf and look pretty. I have been through too much to just sit and look pretty.

I thought my past failures and secrets appeared to be too terrible to be forgiven or forgotten. But when God forgives us, He throws our sins in the sea of forgetfulness, which is as far as the east is from the west; the east never meets the west. God forgave David (a murderer and adulterer) and restored David's relationship with Him. Surely if He did that, God can forgive and cleanse us. It was only after David gave up his way of thinking and living, repented, and admitted his wrongs to God and asked for God's help, forgiveness, and cleansing did he find restoration. David wrote in **Psalms 51:** *"Have mercy on me, O God, because of your unfailing love. Because of your great compassion, blot out the stain of my sins. Wash me clean from my guilt. Purify me from my sin. For I recognized my shameful deeds—they haunt me day and night. Against you and you alone, have I sinned; I have done what is evil in your sight. You will be proved right in what you say, and your judgment against me is just. For I was born a sinner—yes, from the moment my mother conceived me. But you desire honesty from the heart, so you can teach me to be wise in my inmost being.*

Purify me from my sins, and I will be clean; wash me and I will be whiter than snow. Oh, give me back my joy again; you have broken me—now let me rejoice. Don't keep looking at my sins. Remove the stain of my guilt. Create in me a clean heart, O God. Renew a right sprit within me. Do not banish me from your presence, and don't take your Holy Spirit from me. Restore to me again the joy of your salvation and make me willing to obey you."

With a regretful heart, we have to cry out to God as David did about our own sins, and God will do the same for us. In the still of the night, when all is quiet, I cried out to my Father in Heaven, "God help me, forgive me for all I have done and have mercy on me." I knew God could see all things and how this was my time to change. God has given us the courage and strength to endure all things that may come our way. We ask the Lord to carry us when we are unable to walk this path of life, for this battle is a struggle and a constant fight to do the things that are right. We humbly ask, "Oh God, keep us in your precious sight as we open ourselves up to thee."

David was able to really see himself and the wrong that brought him to a state of repentance. God will point out the things about us that He wants us to change. He is willing to take away the behavior that is keeping us in bondage. Sometimes when things are taken from our lives quickly or abruptly, we have to learn to live without that thing or person. Sometimes our old negative behavior traits were like old friends or family members. And when God removes those defects of character, we need to learn how to live without that crutch. When Jesus healed the blind beggar, his lifestyle changed. He could no longer sit before the synagogue begging for his living. He had to learn to live without being blind. Yes, he was healed, but his healing brought about a whole new set of circumstances. Maybe he had to learn a trade and go to work, but I'm sure he could no longer make his living the way he was accustomed to doing; he had to give up a lifestyle. And that is a process!

It doesn't matter if the behavior or defect is negative or even hurtful; it is human nature to mourn the loss of something we are accustomed to having around. We can learn how to live again with the help of the Holy Spirit. When we are ready, we may pray something like the following taken from the book of Alcoholics Anonymous (p76): *"My Creator, I am now willing that you should have all of me, good and bad. I pray that you now remove from me every single defect of character, which stands in the way of my usefulness to you and my fellows. Grant me strength, as I go out from here, to do your bidding, Amen."*

We keep in mind that if God removes the defects in our character He will replace them with His gifts—love, peace, faith, forgiveness, and joy—that are far more valuable than what we had. God does not take away anything without replacing it with something much better than what we thought we had. And there are times He doesn't replace; it just needs to go, to be removed!

CHAPTER EIGHT
"UNFINISHED BUSINESS"

"If you forgive those who sin against you, your heavenly Father will forgive you. But if you refuse to forgive others, your Father will not forgive your sins" **(Matt. 6:14–15; NL).**

Why is forgiveness so important to running this race of life? Why does God want us to forgive so badly? Unforgiveness rots our souls and keeps us from truly experiencing the richness and blessings of God in our lives. Forgiveness can take care of unfinished business.

Forgiveness is hard because it appears that we are letting the person off the hook for what he or she has done to us. The torment is in the fact that we believe that forgiveness allows that person to go unpunished. After the hurt, desertion, abandonment, violation, rejection, and betrayal he or she has caused, he or she is permitted to go scot-free. This type of thinking makes it hard and almost impossible to handle or find forgiveness. This is why we need God in our lives; we can't do it without Him.

No matter what negative experiences we endure in life, true forgiveness is an important part of our recovery process. Forgiveness cleans up unfinished business or deficient affairs and is an important and painful step in the process of healing. Consequently, there is no way we can live this life without the granted opportunity to forgive. If we live long enough, the opportunity for forgiveness will present itself to us. My greatest challenges and growth in God came through opportunities to forgive. *"Then Peter came to him and asked, 'Lord, how often should I forgive someone who sins against me? Seven times?' 'No!' Jesus replied, 'Seventy times seven!'"* **(Matt. 18:21–22).** This statement alone gives us ample opportunity for forgiveness.

Aren't you glad that God is not like us? God said that He will forgive all our sins and heal all our diseases. But we have to deal with this flesh, and the flesh finds it hard to get past anger and bitterness toward those who mistreat and/or abuse us. Holding on to unforgiveness from our past hurts keeps us stuck in the past and prevents us from moving ahead and growing closer to God. God wants us to know what forgiveness means and how important it is to our lives. **Mark 11:25:** *"But when you are praying, first forgive anyone you are holding a grudge against, so that your Father in heaven will forgive your sins, too."* When we ask God's forgiveness for our personal shortcomings and sins, it is hypocritical if we are not willing to forgive others. Meaning we are not living what we say we believe. It is not only hypocritical; it is also selfish and self-destructive not to be willing to forgive. Blessed are those who are merciful, for they will be shown mercy (Matt. 5:7). We never know when our chance for mercy and forgiveness will come.

Unforgiveness keeps us focused on the pain or the wrong that was done to us. It's like having an instant replay button that we press over and over again to replay the harm done and rehash the pain, keeping it fresh in our minds and spirits. Unforgiveness pulls the scab off the sore when it tries to heal and starts the bleeding all over again. The action of forgiveness is a step toward healing; it is a physical and spiritual release. Forgiveness says, "Cease! Stop! Come to an end! It's finished!" When our Savior died on the cross, the last words He said were, "It is finished."

Forgiveness also says, "Stop blaming," "Stop the resentment," and "Stop the demand of a debt, penalty, or payment." Forgiveness is to grant pardon and release from punishment. I am glad Jesus paid it all! He took our punishment and gave us forgiveness as a gift. He took my place on death row although I was guilty as charged. What an example of forgiveness for us to live by that through Jesus there is no sin too big or awful for God to forgive! He can heal all our diseases and forgive all our sins. I am convinced that God wants forgiveness to be a part of our character and lifestyle. Unforgiveness is a character defect that juiced my addiction. I had a long list of people to get high at or refused to forgive, and I could not find peace until I found forgiveness.

In addition, when we think we have forgiven a person, we may need to look a little closer. Some people in the church are able to put on such a sweet soft gentle persona and are hiding bitterness and unforgiveness in their hearts. Maybe just in our words have we forgiven, but when we come in contact with that person, noticeable signs or changes take place in our bodies that confirm the fact that we have not forgiven. I have physical signs; for example, I notice my heart starts to beat faster or my breathing increases. We can say that we have forgiven—actually we can say anything—but sometimes actions speak louder than words.

If another individual can change my attitude, actions, or appearance just by being in his or her presence, something is wrong. In **Ephesians 4:31–32,** God says, *"Get rid of all bitterness, rage, anger, harsh words, slander, as well as all types of malicious behavior. Instead, be kind to each other, tenderhearted, forgiving one another, just as God through Christ has forgiven you."*

When we learn to let go of resentment through forgiveness, we are putting a stop to that person, place, or thing from holding the accountability for our sadness or happiness. In the Kingdom of God, there are spiritual principles that we must live by, and forgiveness is one of those principles. Therefore, unforgiveness in our lives can stand in the way of our blessings and our freedom. It stands in the way of me rising up to Kingdom living.

What an order! But remember we have an example in Jesus about forgiveness. Jesus knows how we feel because He became flesh for us. He walked this earth as we do. He could smell what we smell. He saw through our eyes, heard what we hear, felt what we feel, and He has tasted what we taste. Jesus was God and man. He was tempted in all ways (the pride of life, lust of the flesh, and lust of the eye), but He did not sin. Jesus remains our perfect example even today.

Jesus was betrayed by men close to Him and those He came to save, but He stayed focused with the purpose for which He came to earth. What a man! Even on the cross, Jesus said to the Father, "Forgive them!" In **Luke 23:34**, Jesus said, *"Father, forgive these people because they don't know what they are doing."* I thank God that for at this appointed time, at that request, at that moment, forgiveness was released to me and to the world. Forgiveness went out to the past, present, and future. We can have salvation no matter who we are or what we have done. Because we all fall short of the glory of God, meaning that we have all sinned. So when we refuse to forgive, we choose to live in bondage.

Forgiveness can be a long hard process that many of us fail to comprehend. Some may even refuse to try because of the pain that comes with it, but HEALING HURTS. Oh, God, I am glad that Jesus knows what betrayal feels like so that He can help us.

The willingness and ability to forgive takes us into a life of peace and freedom. I believe God is so concerned about His people that in the healing process our responsibility is to help others to heal also. We have to come to the point of being willing to forgive as well as being forgiven. Forgiveness releases others that we hold hostage in our minds, and it frees them from the penalty of the harm they have caused.

My greatest test of forgiveness came with a certain man in my life who hurt me so badly that I just didn't know if I could recover—a hurt that almost took me out, a hurt that almost caused me to give up on life. Until I met Jesus, forgiveness was not something I would choose to practice. You see, I trusted this man, and he betrayed me terribly. This betrayal affected everything and everyone in my life, especially my children.

In 1990, while attending a support group meeting for my addiction, I met a man who was very crafty and smooth in his conversation and his mannerisms. Although I had made it to a recovery program, I was still seeking love and attention from the wrong people. He was a well-dressed handsome man and an excellent conversationalist. So of course he was able to gain my attention. I thought he had purpose and goals in his life. I believed he was going somewhere in life, and I felt I had to jump on this train because I was so tired of going nowhere, so why not? We began to date. I worked as his secretary in a business that he was trying to get off the ground. After one year of dating, we were so in love that we decided to get married. We were so in love that I was floating on a cloud, and I believed that we were the happiest couple in the world. Again I was lost in my fantasy world, and my Prince Charming clouded my judgment. I was convinced that we would be married for the rest of our lives. We started to do positive things together. We operated our own business, purchased our own home, purchased new cars, and planned for our future.

At that time, I <u>had not</u> accepted Jesus in my life, and I don't believe my new husband had either. It was really not something we talked about. I recognize now that this was the opening for the devil to have his way in our lives. We opened the door for satan to come in and have his way, to kill, steal, and destroy as he intends. God was not first in our marriage or our family; materialism was. I had three children from a prior marriage, two daughters and a son. After approximately one year of marriage, things began to change for the worse. Unresolved issues can tear down anything if we let them; the devil uses unresolved issues that we are afraid to touch or look at to try to destroy us.

Mental and emotional sores, scars, hurts, and pains from both of our pasts ran all over our lives and actually took over. We carried the painful memories from our pasts over into our relationship and covered them up so well with stuff. Consequently, scars, cuts, and bruises that are covered up don't heal well; they have to be uncovered. Furthermore, it is like putting a Band-Aid on an open wound or broken bone. Some wounds have to heal from the inside out. If certain wounds are closed up before they have healed properly on the inside, it will cause infection. The wound will look healed on the outside but leaves the inside to rot away. Additionally, just because it looks well on the outside does not mean it's healed on the inside.

Sometimes what we think is a sound choice can be a mistake that can change our lives forever. How painful and devastating it was for me and my loved ones to wake up to the disturbing and hurtful truth that the man I had joined myself to in marriage, the man I wanted to spend the rest of my life with, was not who I perceived him to be, nor was he who he claimed to be. This man that I chose to trust with my children's lives was a phony!

How could this be? I felt that the man I loved and married had just died an unexpected tragic death. What was I going to do? I felt that I had left reality and was living a nightmare! The horrific news I received over the phone had just changed our whole world!

Now, my two daughters were off to Colorado on a band trip with their school when I received a phone call. Little did I know that on the other end of the phone was the most devastating, demoralizing news I would ever receive. The chaperone with my daughters informed me that my thirteen-year-old daughter had just had a miscarriage and was rushed to the hospital. I was in shock because I was totally in the dark to the fact that she was pregnant. I couldn't believe what I was hearing. The chaperone went on to say that she had more foul news to tell me. She went on to say that the man I called my husband was the father of my thirteen-year-old daughter's baby.

At that moment, my heart stopped, and I felt my world fall from under me. My loving husband had been sexually abusing my daughter under my very nose. This malicious spirit of sexual abuse had invaded my life once again; the first time was when I was a child. My innocence was stolen from me by a relative at the age of twelve, and I swore that no one would ever do the same to my children. Therefore, I thought I was protecting them by providing a stable home and family, but without God, without Jesus in our lives, we are all unprotected! But even with God's divine protection, man still has free will.

Well, painfully so, I lost my husband and my family that day in a matter of moments! I realize that my life was one fabrication! My reality was gone! As our whole world fell down around us, I flew to Colorado to get my daughter and bring her home. This was too much for me to bear. How was I supposed to face my daughter and the world? I wanted to die. I was feeling things I had never felt before. I wanted to end it all, literally. Even though the drugs and alcohol were out of my life, life just kept on happening. I knew I could hide behind a drug or a drink of alcohol, but I couldn't give in to drugs and alcohol again.

Most of all, I knew the pain my daughter felt all too well, and I just couldn't bear the fact that she was experiencing that type of devastation, and I couldn't do anything about it. I knew what he had taken from her, and I didn't know how to give it back to her. I was powerless and hopeless; I didn't even know how to get it back for myself.

How was I to give back to her the loss of dignity, self-respect, self-esteem, and the right to be the daughter of the King and so much more that was violated and stripped away from her? How could I mend her brokenness? The only thing I can give to her today is Jesus, who is more than enough; He is our "Healing."

Abuse has existed for a long time, destroying lives and families, as it was for Tamar, her story is found in the Bible (2 Sam. 13). Tamar was a virgin and a beautiful, good, pure, untouched young woman unspoiled by the world (like the innocence of my child). Regretfully so, her innocence and everything that she was and inspired to be was taken away from her by somebody else's lust. The devil tempts us only with what our flesh desires.

After Tamar's perpetrator (her brother) had sex with her, he took away her rights and the future of honor that was expected from her as the daughter of the king. The devil has tried to take away my rights and the rights of my children to inherit the Kingdom of God. But God has made me promises, and He has given us back our rights as His children and given us through Jesus the potential to be all that He wants for us. God has given me great promises for my children, and I receive them all. They will be delivered and set free! My children are saved today, and they have given me beautiful grandchildren. God is a God of second chances!

The topic of sexual abuse is hard to talk about, but what I know is that the pain we share with each other is pain lessened in our lives. We only hope that our courage will offer hope to the hopeless and those living in bondage a way out. The devil has absolutely nothing to hold over my head or my children. Real freedom comes from not having anything to hide. The truth of my life is told not to hurt anybody but to help heal. As a result, HEALING HURTS!

Women and children in this world are being destroyed every day because of abuse, and they are afraid to talk about it. The things we keep in the dark grow and die in the exposure to the "Light." God looks for the root of the problem so it may be removed; He finds the hurt so it can be healed. People of all ages are suffering from their pasts and are stuck in the bondage that the past can bring. Often people are unable to come out of their abuse, which stunts growth emotionally and spiritually although the physical body continues to grow and mature.

In my experience, I believe that there is a hurting child inside of every adult who was abused, whether it was emotionally, sexually, or physically. Inside of every drug addict, there is a child waiting to grow up. That child has been left behind unable to heal, waiting to be rescued, still in pain, needing to be healed. During the time I was abusing drugs, it interrupted my growth emotionally and spiritually. When sexual abuse happens, everybody loses—that is, until the healing starts with Jesus. In most cases, the perpetrators have once been victims themselves, and if the victim does not seek the help necessary, the cycle is repeated in the family. Furthermore, no matter how we try to protect our loved ones, when sexual abuse has been revealed, it is usually too late.

During this awful time of my life, I could not see a way out of my situation. I went from a love/love relationship to a love/hate relationship to a hate/hate relationship with my ex-husband seemingly overnight. Oh God, what was I to do with this love that I had for him? It was a confusing time of my life. Besides living in fear, I was obsessed with the thought of it all. I asked myself, "How did Jesus continue to love in the midst of betrayal?" My life was consumed with the thought of what horrible things this man (I thought I knew) had done to my daughter. I thought about it daily, and when I was not thinking about it, I was dreaming about it. How was I going to get out of this situation? How was I going to help my children? It was eating me alive. I couldn't get the thought or image out of my mind. I talked with anyone who would listen, until they were tired of hearing me. I felt helpless to help my daughter or myself. Because of the legal matters that stood ahead of me, forgiveness was far from my mind. I knew I was angry with God, and as a result, I found myself laying out in my front yard yelling up at God, "How could you allow this to happen?!" I had to blame somebody; I thought God could have stopped it!

Our healing from this situation started on a day when I was given a gold cross on a chain and my first Bible. The Spirit of God led me to read the story about Job. Well, I started to read how he lost so much and how Job lost it so quickly and drastically. I could relate to the loss and despair that Job went through. Although his pain was far greater than mine, it was bad enough for me! My pain at the time was so intense and cut so deeply that I couldn't take time to read through the whole story of Job. After reading about his losses and pain, I quickly turned to the end of the book of Job to see how this story was gonna turn out! I needed hope. I had none, and I needed it right away! I desperately needed to know that it was going to be all right. I was comforted to know that God blessed Job more than before; there was hope!

Although I started to see a glimmer of hope, I still had unforgiveness in my heart. I wanted revenge. I thought God could not possibly let this man off the hook by simply forgiving him, but God knows how to reach us. He knows how to work things together for our good. I recall a conversation I had with another woman in my support group who knew my story and what my family and I had been through. She asked me what would happen if this man who did this horrible thing went to heaven. I said, "Oh, no! You have got to be kidding! He cannot go to heaven after what he did!" She replied, "Oh, yes, he can; all he has to do is what you have done: repent, accept Jesus, and ask God for forgiveness." (sin is sin.) I was so disturbed about this man going to heaven and God making it so easy for him. She went on to say, "So, what are you going to do in heaven? Walk around all day with resentment?" Well, I figured as long as God did not put my mansion next to his I would be okay. But later I thought about what she said. What would I do when I got to heaven and he was there? This conversation led me to open up to a forgiving spirit and come to grips with the fact that I cannot live in heaven with unforgiveness in my heart. I couldn't bear the thought of this man making it and me being lost to unforgiveness, so I had to reevaluate.

I could not take this hatred to heaven with me, so something had to change. Like I said, forgiveness is a Kingdom principle, and hatred is not. Forgiveness is a code that I have to try to teach my children for their survival. God wants us to love others as he has loved us, and because of the principle of forgiveness, my children and I have been able to move on with our lives. I have asked for their forgiveness, and I have been able to forgive myself and receive God's forgiveness most of all, which puts us in peace with each other. But in some cases, forgiveness does not mean that we accept that person back into our lives; we let them go with peace!

God honors relationships. Forgiveness brought my family back together, and my children and I have special relationships. Forgiveness has the power to bind things together, to mend brokenness, and to mend relationships. God's forgiveness through Christ brought mankind into a relationship with Him. Forgiveness has the power to birth new beginnings when it's real and genuine. God's forgiveness gives us the power and ability to forgive and to live a lifestyle of forgiveness. The power of peace comes from forgiveness as we work toward our goal of having peace with God, ourselves, and others. It is not so much of what happens to us in this world that keeps us in bondage, but how we choose to respond to it that kills us or frees us.

Forgiveness is to grant pardon! To release the prisoner! To release someone from punishment! Glory to God, in spite of myself, Christ took my place on death row! Although I was guilty of my sins, Jesus took it all, and God found me not guilty! And He wants us to display the same example of mercy and grace to others. We are to hold back some things that we know others deserve who have harmed us, and we give the favor of things we know they don't deserve, and we will receive these same blessings in our lives. We finish our business, leaving nothing undone.

CHAPTER NINE
"CLEAN UP YOUR MESS"

"If someone says, 'I love God,' but hates a Christian brother or sister, that person is a liar; for if we don't love people we can see, how can we love God, who we have not seen?" **(1 John 4:20).**

I have not always been the victim; I have experienced both sides of the coin. I admit remorsefully that I have hurt many people because of my actions, behavior, and choices. As a result, I left a trail of hurting people behind me, and that included my children and family. My brother Kenneth asked me one day, after a long period of drug use, "Sis, when does it all stop? Where does the madness all end?" I had no answer for him because I had no idea. When I gave his question some consideration, I thought it would all end in death. I could not see any other way.

Today, I acknowledge that part of my healing is to go back and help others to heal. I have to clean up my mess on my side of the street. This is done by making things right through love. We have to stop leaving our wounded on the battlefield to die. The damage has to be repaired in order for the healing to take place. One person who needed my help most of all was me. I was told that if I could find healing for myself, then it would increase the chances for my loved ones to heal.

It is important that we deal with ourselves as lovingly as we would others. We love thy neighbor as we love ourselves. As I addressed myself, I started to know that God's love for me was unfailing. His love is constant, always there, never ends; it's everywhere I go and in everything around me. His love covers me and loves me when I am right or wrong. God's love is powerful enough to guide, protect, comfort, and keep me day and night. It is a love that has no break in it. It's a love that is as solid as a rock; it never quits, never stops, and is faithful unto death. What a love! Hallelujah! As long as we are in God's hands, nothing can separate us. We can do all things through His strength.

The apostle Paul wrote the most encouraging words found in the Bible in **Romans 8:38–39:** *"And I am convinced that nothing can ever separate us from His love. Death can't and life can't. The angels can't and the demons can't. Our fears for today, our worries about tomorrow, and even the powers of hell can't keep God's love away. Whether we are high above the sky or in the deepest ocean, nothing in all creation will ever be able* *to separate us from the love of God that is revealed in Christ Jesus our Lord."*

God says that love conquers all things because it is the greatest gift of all. Love is the main ingredient of the healing process. Love can heal addictions and free us from bondage. Our goal is to live in harmony with God, ourselves, and other people; this is "love." And one way to live in harmony is to make things right by repairing the damage that we have done. We are all <u>called by God</u> to love others by walking in love and having the character of love. Sometimes we may wonder what we are called to do, but if you look closely, you will see the "universal call," which is to "love." **1 Corinthians 13:4** says, *"Love suffers long and is kind; love does not envy; love does not parade itself, is not puffed up; does not behave rudely, does not seek its own, is not provoked, thinks no evil; does not rejoice in iniquity, but rejoices in the truth; bears all things, believes all things, hopes all things, endures all things"* (New King James Version). And we know that when this life is over, love will outlast everything, because God is love. This is actually a description of His love for us, and without this type of love what we have means nothing.

Repairing the brokenness is important to my sobriety. Restitution can be a long process, but I started making repairs in my life for things that I had broken during my active addiction. First, I asked the forgiveness of my mother and my children and started to live a sober life. After making amends to them, I started to make one to myself, and I started with writing a letter. I would like to share the words of my letter with you: ***"Dear Patricia, I have been wrong toward you in the past. I have made decisions that caused you to have less than what God wants for you. I have caused you pain and loss, talked badly about you, and put you down. Most of all, I have not loved you as God wants me to. I have neglected you physically and spiritually. I have led you in to areas that were dangerous for you and your children. Please forgive me for all that I have caused you in your life. And please know that you are a virtuous woman, and I will from this day forward treat you with the respect and dignity that you truly deserve in being the daughter of the King. I love you forever. Signed, Patricia."***

If you are in need of healing from abuse that you have caused yourself, I urge you to take time and write your own letter of amends and watch the anointing of God do wonders in starting to put you back together. I had to start speaking life to myself by encouraging myself. I have learned to embrace myself with love and kindness instead of looking for it from others. Today, when or if I get a stroke or compliment from others, it doesn't dictate my day or my self-worth; it's an extracurricular measure because it has already been done by me.

Life is too short to continue to hold grudges and live without harmony and peace with the important people in our lives. On September 11, 2001, we all had a jolt of reality and realized how short life can be when the Twin Towers were destroyed in New York, claiming so many lives. We have to make the best of our lives and our relationships while we have them. Regretfully, sometimes we take people and time for granted, and we miss it when it's gone. It is like water spilled on the ground that we can never retrieve. It's lost forever!

The bondage of addiction in my life separated me from peace, and it is time to have peace in my life. God is able to heal us and the people in our lives that we have harmed, if we are willing to allow Him. Experience says that after any disaster, there is a repairing and rebuilding that has to take place in our lives, whether it is physical or spiritual. The love of God makes this time of putting things back together successful. Through His power, we can love those we find impossible to love and even love those who hurt us so deeply. More so, with God's power, we learn to adjust to the losses in our lives.

Jesus gives us a peace that surpasses all understanding! If we seek peace from God, He will provide it, because He is faithful to what He has promised those who pursue Him. God rewards those who diligently seek Him, meaning we have to stay in the process of healing. God says it is a wonderful thing to live in peace with others. In **Psalms 133**, David gives praise to "unity" after many years of conflict. *"How wonderful it is, how pleasant, when brothers live together in harmony! For harmony is as precious as the fragrant anointing oil that was poured over Aaron's head, that ran down his beard and onto the border of his robe. Harmony is as refreshing as the dew from Mount Hermon that falls on the mountains of Zion. And the Lord has pronounced his blessing, even life forevermore."* **John 4:7–12** says, *"Dear Friends, let us continue to love one another, for love comes from God. Anyone who loves is born of God and knows God. But anyone who does not love does not know God—for God is love. God showed how much he loved us by sending his only son into the world so that we might have eternal life through him. This is real love. It is not that we loved God, but that he loved us and sent his son as a sacrifice to take away our sins. Dear friends, since God loved us that much, we surely ought to love each other. No one has ever seen God, but if we love each other, God lies in us, and his love has been brought to full expression through us."*

We love God by showing love to others, and God will recognize us by the love in our hearts. We may agree that love is believed to be important in this world, but we are expecting a feeling of euphoria or excitement to prove we are in love or being loved. In reality, love is a choice and an action as mentioned above; it is the way we treat people. The problem is that people are not willing to go very far to show love. When a demonstration of love starts to inconvenience us, then problems occur. The Good Samaritan (Luke 10:30–37) gives us an example of how far love goes. The Samaritan, who represented the love of Christ, went all the way with this wounded man. Which proves that when we are loving we are most like Christ. When he saw the wounded man lying on the side of the road dying, he was moved with deep compassion for him. When Jesus found me, I was wounded and dying, and He was moved with pity and love for me. His love went all the way to the cross for my wounds. This is our example of love!

What an order, and I cannot go through with it on my own, not without my Savior. It hurts to love the way God is asking us to. I have often thought, "God, you have got to be kidding; you expect me to do that!" To lift up someone higher than myself is the opposite of what I had been used to doing. The Word of God always challenges us to do better and love more. God is busy trying to make us like Christ. We are not alone. His love hurts, but it heals and builds; it won't destroy us. John 10:10 says we have an enemy, a thief, and his purpose is to steal, kill, and destroy. But Jesus' purpose is to give life in all its fullness, lacking nothing.

God is the source of our love, and without Him in our lives we cannot live as He has called us to do. Jesus loved people into submission and restoration, and He is our example. He is the lover of our souls and the teacher of love. When I accepted Jesus into my heart, the Holy Spirit gave me power to love the same, as He'll do for you. The Holy Spirit continues to make me more and more like Christ daily as I submit to His will. We are given the grace to get things right in our lives. It is a humbling experience to approach another human being with the words, "I was wrong, and this is what I will do to make it right." This is truly a statement and act of love. I had broken relationships in my life that needed mending, and it takes more than just saying, "I'm sorry." It takes action to repair broken relationships. In many cases, just the result of me changing my life helped restore important relationships.

God's love always involves choice and action. The vital question is, "How well do we display our love for God in the choices we make or the actions we take?" We choose to love.

When Jesus went to the cross, His purpose was to clean up the mess of this world. He offered eternal life to a dying world and proclaimed liberty to the captives. It was "real love" Jesus demonstrated when He went to the cross. What do you think He was feeling? The Bible does not declare that Jesus went to the cross smiling and skipping happily because of love. The greatest display of love came with anguish and pain. HEALING HURTS! He went to the cross to bring healing into this world. Without the cross, there would be no way out of the addiction that held me but death. I thank Jesus that the pain of the cross didn't stop Him. Before Jesus went to the cross in **Matthew 26:37–38,** *"He took Peter and Zebedee's two sons, James and John, as He went to pray, and he began to be filled with anguish (grief and sorrow) and deep distress. He told them, 'My soul is crushed with grief to the point of death.'"* The love it took to heal the world was full of anguish, grief, sorrow, and distress. **The love of God heals many.**

The wonderful thing about this miraculous event of passion at the cross is that Jesus was not forced to go; He was not forced to lay down His life for us. He chose to go in obedience to His Father's will. The point here is that choice and action moves much further than what I feel for you. When Jesus was here on earth, He was not only God but He was also a man wrapped in flesh. Furthermore, Jesus had to fulfill the purpose in spite of what His feelings were. It was "love" that kept Him on the cross! It was God that kept Him on the cross! The greatest display of love is when we can lay down our lives for a friend. This love is demonstrated even as we share our experiences, strengths, and hopes.

When we are involved in the search for a love that only makes us feel good, we are into selfishness, and that is the exact opposite of God's love. A self-centered person cannot truly love because he or she is always concerned about himself or herself, and that was me for many years. What about me? I have asked this question various times, "What about me?" The response was, "What about you?" I was told that it's not about me; it is all about God and His purpose for me. Every trial that I have suffered and made it through was not even about me; it was for someone else. God brought me through so I can tell you that you can make it too!

God's love and forgiveness gives us freedom to take our eyes off ourselves and meet the needs of others. Christ's sacrifice established His love for us. And in return, I lay my life out to you in love, by putting myself into this book, hoping that it will help lead someone into a better understanding and relationship with God.

Jesus had to take His eyes off of His anguish and pain and put His focus totally on God to follow through with the Master's plan. He said, "If it is Thy will, let Thy will be done." We needed a way to God; we needed a Savior, and that was the purpose of Jesus, to reveal the Father to us.

If God is not our teacher when it comes to love, we are just toying with somebody's life that will only lead to unnecessary pain and suffering. Without God, we cannot have a real, sincere, and genuine love. **Romans 12:9–10** says, *"Don't pretend that you love others. Really love them. Hate what is wrong, stand on the side of the good. Love each other with genuine affection and take delight in honoring each other."* Genuine love is healing, and healing love is action and choice. It demands our time, money, and personal involvement, not just empty words that are irrelevant to the situation at hand. For example, I cannot repair a financial situation with only kind words. A financial amends takes money! We have to use God's wisdom to lead us to the needs we can meet in this world.

1 Peter 1:21–22: *"Through Christ you have come to trust in God. And because God raised Christ from the dead and gave him great glory, your faith and hope can be placed confidently in God. Now you can have sincere love for each other as brothers and sisters, because you were cleansed from your sins when you accepted the truth of the Good News. So see to it that you really do love each other intensely* [great seriousness] *with all your hearts."* We are to make it our business to love each other, because without love nothing stands. I ran from the very thing that I wanted most in my life, "love." Love allows us to go back and mend the things that we have broken, clean up the mess, and call help for the wounded people we have left behind lying on the side of the road. We can now speak life to the dead because the same Spirit that raised Jesus operates in us.

CHAPTER TEN
"KEEP YOURSELF IN CHECK"

1 Timothy 4:16 (New Living): *"Keep a close watch on yourself and on your teaching. Stay true to what is right and God will save you and those who hear you."*

I have a daily reprieve that depends on the preservation of my spiritual condition. I have to continue to feed my spiritual self to maintain and receive this lifestyle that God wants for me. The Holy Spirit helps me keep myself in check daily by pointing out things that need to change by confronting myself. I have to stay vigilant at looking at my actions, attitudes, relationships, and myself in order to live a sober life.

This is a preventive action that's not easy but considered necessary because I don't want to go back to my past. Lot's wife looked back to see the city of Sodom burning; some say she was clinging to her past, and she was unwilling to let go completely. I don't know why she really looked back, but I do know God told her not to look back. So consequently, she was turned into a pillar of salt or otherwise destroyed. Her unresolved issues and her inability to let go of the past may have caused her to look back instead of forward to the new life that God had in store for her. The fear of change and the unknown kept me stuck in the past, looking back, and using drugs and alcohol for comfort and the illusion of peace.

For many years, I used drugs and drank alcohol because of what was missing in my life or resentment that I carried. In some cases, I swore that if it took me a lifetime I would get revenge. At the present time, for me to hold on to old behavior is to flirt with death. It is to play "Russian roulette" with my life to carry anger, resentment, or unforgiveness, because they can all become reasons for me to use drugs and alcohol again. As long as I keep myself in check, I can rid myself of these stumbling blocks and not allow anything to build up to the point of using drugs or alcohol. Life became so much easier for me when I took hold of the idea that the only person I am capable of changing is myself, and your opinion of me is not my business!

Many work hard to forget the past. The truth is that we cannot totally forget what we have been through. All of the people, events, and experiences from my past play a part in who I am today. "Forgetting those things that are behind us" implies that we don't let our past dictate our lives or live in the past. One important thing about the past is that we get to a point where we don't regret it, but understand it. We learn how to use our past and we can see how the experiences we have had can help others. Most important, we stop living in the past and start living in the here and now with anticipation for the future. The only reason we look back into our past is to learn from it, share it, and teach from it. My freedom and healing in Christ allows me to purposely reach back to get something that will help others make it through their pain. At one time, my past controlled me—not anymore. I go back only when it is necessary to help others come out.

I have to remain diligent in my efforts of seeking God and what He wants in my life, because this is how I will receive the rewards He has for me. God gives us an example of the persistent widow in Luke 18:1–9. She didn't give up; in spite of the circumstances, she was determined to get her fair share. We too can be persistent in our efforts by living for God day after day and pressing toward the mark of the "High Calling." We evaluate our lives to be more like Christ, who is the "High Calling." We see where our lives don't measure up, and we become willing to allow God to change us. We cannot give up; we have to hold on to God's promised word with faith that He fulfills His promises. "Blessed is She, Blessed is He that believes for there shall be a performance or fulfillment of those things told them by the Lord" (Luke 1:45). Our belief can bring blessings into our lives.

A productive life calls for balance, and the wholeness that comes from this balance includes spiritual, relational, physical, mental, and economical components. If I am not careful, my self-defeating behaviors can prevent that balance from happening and interfere in my getting closer to God, which will eventually lead back to drug use. Addiction affects every area of life. In addition, success in Christ comes from staying teachable and obedient to His ways. Submission will keep us out of a lot of unnecessary trouble in our lives. We stop justifying and rationalizing our wrongs and pray for guidance through the Holy Spirit.

My new lifestyle today has become a living amends. It is one way of repairing relationships with my family, myself, the world, and God. I am on my way somewhere that only God knows. He can lead us down paths that no one else knows are there and equip us to do things no one else has ever done! Today I am headed in a direction that's best for me; it's God's way! I would have never believed over sixteen years ago, the crack addict I was, that God would be doing the things He is doing in me. All I have to do is follow the direction of the Holy Spirit because anything else leads to destruction. The road I am on now is narrow, and I can't get lost; this road (way of life) has many stop signs for me (e.g., stop drinking, stop doing drugs, stop fornicating, stop lying, stop cheating, stop hurting others, etc.), and they are all in place to help me live a quality life. The old road was wide with plenty of room to get lost, and I did. I could do anything I wanted to, and most of the time, my "want to" led to hell in my life. I had no stop signs on this road; I was free to go to hell! And I was on a fast train to hell, and I didn't know how to make it stop! **Proverbs 14:12**, *"There is a path before each person that seems right, but it ends in death."*

My past was a journey that kept me walking in one big vicious circle until I met Jesus. I was wandering around in my own wilderness because of disobedience. Jesus came into my personal hell and rescued me! He freed me from the prison I made for myself, and His Spirit continues to guide, convict, and teach me the right way. **Psalms 143:10–11,** *"Teach me to do your will for you are my God. May your gracious Spirit lead me forward on a firm footing."* **Psalms 25:4–5,** *"Show me the path where I should walk, O Lord; point out the right road for me to follow. Lead me by your truth and teach me, for you are the God who saves me. All day long I put my hope in you."* I am nothing without the Lord in my life; my hope is in Him.

As a result, God continues to work on my character. He is concerned about our character, because our character is what we operate out of daily. God has given us instructions on how to live because He is concerned about how we are living, which includes how we treat others. I wasted so much time hating and being totally consumed with my drug and myself. The only reason I would look to others was for my own need and with the question, "What can you do for me, or what have you done for me lately?" Now I know that anyone who even came in contact with me was at risk. And if you were not a part of what I was doing, I had no need for you. I kept people around me who helped to keep me in denial because they were just like me. All my associates and so-called friends were drug users or drug dealers, and we all looked the same so it was hard to see the insanity until I went around someone who was supposed to be normal.

Time is precious, and I do not want to waste one more minute, hour, day, month, or year holding resentment or fear or doing the wrong thing and doing it with the wrong people. The psalmist says that our days are like pouring water on the ground; we cannot pick it up, and it's gone forever. After this life is over, we just don't get another chance; this is it, baby! What you see is what you get! So each day is new and full of new grace and mercy from God. We learn to live life as a gift, one day at a time. And part of my healing is to continue to let the Holy Spirit keep me in check daily. Recovering from my drug addiction has not been easy, and it most certainly requires keeping in step with the Holy Spirit. I believe if we can do this, after this race has been run, when it's all over, when it's all said and done, there will be no regrets or saying, "I wish I had ..."

The Bible serves as our spiritual mirror. It is the only thing we need to compare our lives to. **James 2:23–25** says, *"And remember, it is a message to obey, not just to listen to. If you don't obey, you are only fooling yourself. For if you just listen and don't obey, it is like looking at your face in a mirror but doing nothing to improve your appearance. You see yourself, walk away, and forget what you look like."* We look in the mirror to make changes or improvements to what we see. As we read the Bible daily, we are constantly looking in the mirror, but when I see my flaws, it is to correct, not to justify. It is insanity to look and see but do nothing.

Denial can keep me from seeing, but checking myself on a regular basis will keep me out of denial. When I keep myself in check, I can never forget what I look like, and the Holy Spirit challenges me to change. God uses the people in my life to challenge me to continue to correct my ways. My grandchildren have never seen me high on drugs or even smoke a cigarette; what a miracle! My love for my grandchildren challenges me to do the best I can to stay sober. I desire to leave behind an example they can follow. I want to leave them something useful instead of memories of a dead drug addict!

And I can do this, if I keep looking steadily into God's perfect law, the law that sets us free. If we do what He says and don't forget what we hear, then God blesses us for doing so. So check yourself! When you look into the mirror, what reflection do you see? Are you being true to yourself? Only you and God know the truth. Well remember, "To thy own self be true!" We have to be sincerely honest with ourselves and remember to look at the good things about us as well. It's okay to look in the mirror and like what you see. We have to keep a balance of humility in our lives by accepting who we are, the good and the not so good. Honesty has been the antidote to my sick mind. I tell you, my healing has been a process of renewing my mind. We have to know who we are in Christ and when we recognize areas that need to change, change them! Looking into the mirror keeps us free, and where the Spirit of the Lord is, there is freedom. If Jesus is the building block of our character, we are truly free!

One morning, the Holy Spirit awakened me early and led me to write down a set of instructions so I wouldn't forget them. He said, "God wants you to have the 'Character of Faith,' and that is to live a lifestyle where His glory is able to shine through you to draw people to Him, and talk to others about the Character of Faith." My character is what others will see and experience about me. The "character of faith" is to put Jesus first in my coming and going. Furthermore, Jesus said, "If I be lifted up I will draw all men unto me." When people look at you, what do they see? Can they see Jesus? Is Jesus lifted up in your life?

I remember times during my drug addiction that my body would exude the fragrance of whatever drug or alcohol I had been using. When I walked into a room, the people there knew I had been smoking marijuana or drinking alcohol because they could smell it. Today I want the fragrance of love to shine through my pores instead of alcohol and drugs. The fragrance of God's anointing and the sweet smell of the Holy Spirit will shine through my life. It is a fragrance like no other! My gratitude is a worship and praise to God for saving a wreck like me. Our praise reaches God's nostrils as the sweet-smelling perfume that Mary used to anoint Jesus before He went to the cross (**Mark 14:1–9**).

Her gratitude was shown in this action for all Jesus had done for her. This was her praise to Him, and she gave Him the best she had. (Thousands of dollars' worth of perfume was poured over His body at one time. Of course, those who were watching thought she went a little overboard.) The Bible says nothing of Jesus bathing before He went to the cross. Therefore, as He hung on the cross, I imagine that sweet smell of praise pierced the nose of our Lord God, and He was reminded of her great display of gratitude for all He had done. As a result, when I praise God with a grateful attitude for what He has done, it too is like a sweet aroma to Him. If I can stay grateful, I can stay out of worrying about the "what if's" in life because I will know that my God is in charge and gratitude builds our character.

When we have the character of faith, we have the character of Christ because He is faith. We wear our character like clothes; we put on the right behavior that pleases God. Others will see our behavior or our character similar to how they see the clothing we wear; our clothes tell a great deal about us. **Colossians 3:12–14,** *"Since God chose you to be the holy people whom he loves, you must clothe yourselves with tenderhearted mercy, kindness, humility, gentleness, and patience. You must make allowance for each other's faults and forgive the person who offends you. Remember, the Lord forgave you, so you must forgive others. And the most important piece of clothing you must wear is love."*

We stop comparing ourselves to other people and start measuring up to who Christ says we are. This is the character of faith, because Jesus is Faith, and without "Faith" it is impossible to please God. The character of faith is living by love and obedience to the Word of God and having a heart for His purpose. When I keep myself in check, it means I am under the influence of the Holy Spirit instead of alcohol and drugs or some other destructive power. **Ephesians 5:17–18,** *"Don't act thoughtlessly, but try* *to understand what the Lord wants you to do. Don't be drunk with wine, because that will ruin your life. Instead, let the Holy Spirit fill and control you.*" I had a problem long before I started to use drugs. The emptiness inside of me as a child, wondering where I fit in, caused me to try to fill that emptiness with whatever I could. It started with candy, but as I grew up, my "soul fillers" started to change to more destructive things like sex, men, and drugs, not knowing that God is the only thing that can fill me. He is my Filler today.

Romans 1:17 says, *"The Just shall live by faith,"* and this is living as if God is telling the truth. We can be guilty of performing certain acts to make it appear as if we are living by faith, but God sees our hearts as well as what we do. When I keep myself in check, I do a heart check because it is hard to tell what is lurking in there. **Matthew 12: 34b-35,** *"For whatever is in your heart determines what you say. A good person produces good words from a good heart, and an evil person produces evil words from an evil heart."*

God knows everything about us. He knows what we will think before we think it; He knows what we will say before we say it. He knows our motives, and our motives are just as important to Him as our actions because our motives concern the heart, and the heart involves the character of the man or the woman. Some of us have heart trouble, and our heartbeat is off, and it is only God who can change such a delicate thing as our heart. The beat of our heart is the center of our existence. Not only does God change the beat of our heart, He gives us a new heart, one that is genuine with genuine motives. **Ezekiel 36:25-27,** *"Then I will sprinkle clean water on you and you will be clean. Your filth will be washed away, and you will no longer worship idols. And I will give you a new heart with new and right desires, and I will put a new spirit in you. I will take out your stony heart of sin and give you a new, obedient heart. And I will put my Spirit in you so you will obey my laws and do whatever I command."*

We don't want to be hypocrites hiding our character with a mask of religious acts; the masks have to go. When I was using cocaine, it was easy to hide behind a mask and pretend to be whoever I wanted to be for the moment. The mask has to go; time is precious, and it is time to be real with myself. I must continue to change and allow Jesus to transform me from the inside out. God is concerned about our insides, because whatever is going on inside of us dictates what happens on the outside. **1 Peter 3:3–4** says, *"Don't be concerned about the outward beauty that depends on fancy hairstyles, expensive jewelry, or beautiful clothes. You should be known for the beauty that comes from within,* (heart) *the unfading beauty of a gentle and quiet spirit, which is so precious to God."*

My worth was always external, and that is why I could never measure up or find where I fit in. The most important lesson is to find my worth within. Now, don't take me wrong, looking the best I can is important to me. Because there were days in my drug use that the cocaine controlled me to the point that it would not let me eat, sleep, or bathe. I would wear the same clothes for days and sometimes two pairs of pants at the same time because I only weighed about ninety-eight pounds. The extra clothes gave me the appearance of extra weight. So each day I am blessed to wake up and take care of my basic needs like bathing, brushing my teeth, eating, and putting on a set of clean clothing; that alone is a miracle! But my worth is not tied up in that alone; my value is in who God says I am, not the worth of my stuff.

When we keep ourselves under God's spotlight, we are able to see things we couldn't see in the dark. This kind of daily personal inventory allows us to see patterns that we can put an end to before they become too much to handle. This keeps me from boxing myself into a corner from which the only way out is for me to use drugs. One thing I noticed about myself was that I was repeating some of the same mistakes over and over again without the use of drugs or alcohol. I have become fed **up** with this repetitious cycle of insanity in my life in expecting something different. I look forward to making new mistakes instead of the same ones. The use of alcohol and drugs can cause this type of insanity, but sometimes in the situations life can present to us, we can find ourselves echoing the same cycles. What plagues us most of all is that we have simple living problems, and God can teach us how to live. The Bible is a set of instructions on how to live. I can keep myself from returning to insanity by making a simple choice not to go back. To go back to my addiction would be like a dog eating its own vomit!

Jesus has given us guidelines for living this life in the character of faith. Living the principles of Kingdom life is described best in what is known as the Beatitudes found in Matthew chapter five. When we operate in decisions or choices that agree with God's Word, we reap a blessed and healed life; that's a promise! Actually, we only have two choices: we can either choose to live or die. We must choose to live by God's Word, which offers so much hope for us today and eternally. For me to choose drugs and alcohol today is choosing death and turning my back on God after all He has done for me.

My pride kept me living in bondage and addiction for many years because it wouldn't let me ask for help. I have to keep watch on the pride that comes up in my life, because pride will not let me see what is right about me; it will not let me see the truth. Pride disguises itself in different ways that keep us sick. Pride keeps me focused on me in a selfish way. Pride doesn't deal with healing; it deals with appearance. According to Kingdom principles, where there is an absence of pride and personal vanity, there is a nourishing reliance on God. So we are warned to not live as fools, because it is insane. A fool cannot comprehend the truth when he or she hears it, and a fool cannot comprehend the truth about himself or herself. More than that, without admitting the truth, healing cannot take place. **Proverbs 29:23,** *"Pride ends in humiliation, while humility brings honor."*

Pride will not let us see what is right in front of our faces! We can become spiritually blind, which is the main reason we need Jesus; He came to give sight to the blind. Part of the process of being dependent on God is admitting our own lack and giving ourselves completely to God. I confess that I am nothing without God, and I can do all things through Christ who lives in me. It is Him who does a great work through me. Today I know that there is no failing in my God; therefore, if He lives in me, then there is no failing in me.

I acknowledge the overwhelming mistakes that I have made in my life, and I feel sad and broken over the wrong things that I have done. As a result, in this healing process, God wants my heart right with Him. The process of keeping myself in check—staying aware of where I am, who I am, and who I'm with—helps me live a life of recovery. Life, no matter how it comes, is much better without the use of drugs and alcohol. I understand one important fact, and that is, we reap what we sow. If I want peace in my life, chances are I need to sow peace; what a concept! For me, drug addiction did not bring peace, only discard and destruction. As I walk this life of recovery and restoration, I have found one thing that the people with quality recovery have in common: They have found peace in their lives. This is a "peace" that only comes from the acknowledged existence of a power greater than themselves. I believe that God is that power. I once heard a man who was into his thirtieth year of sobriety from alcohol and drugs say, "There are no big deals anymore." Living as a drug addict, everything is a big deal and a big enough excuse to use drugs.

In Christ, we can find peace even after we have caused so much havoc in our lives and the lives of others too. God calls us to live in peace (1 Cor. 7:15). My pastor said, "When we give up the ability to reason with each other, then there is no peace, and you can bet that the devil is somewhere in the camp, because he is the author of confusion." If we stay teachable, we can keep the ability to work things out in our lives; this is why we keep ourselves in check. We learn that if we can accept life on life's terms, it is the key to solving our problems today. We keep our focus on us and what we need to change about ourselves, because if there is one thing we have the power to change, it is us.

Peace in our lives gives us a quiet-calm character, and this doesn't mean being a doormat that others walk on each day in order to be a good Christian. Operating in peace, we are able to think before we respond to life situations. Most of my life and especially when I was high on drugs, I reacted to most situations instead of responding because I was compulsive. Our responses to the trials of life can determine our survival. We want a character of extreme self-control that is directed by the Holy Spirit. The gift of self-control gives me the power of choice to say no when I need to say no and say yes at the right time.

Our character should hunger and thirst for righteousness. My body, mind, and soul craved and thirsted for cocaine and many other destructive desires. I wouldn't stop until I got what I wanted. Now God wants that same desire from me for Him and in doing what is right. **Psalms 42:2–3,** *"As the deer pants for streams of water, so I long for you, O God. I thirst for God, the living God. When can I come and stand before him?"* This draws me nearer to my Lord, and our relationship becomes more intimate. As this happens, there is no room for the use of drugs. As I learn to live without my addiction, I learn to copy God's ways and turn from my own ways and what the world thinks is best for me. We seek God's righteousness instead of our own accomplishments. **Proverbs 3:5–6,** *"Trust in the Lord with all your heart; do not depend on your own understanding. Seek his will in all you do, and he will direct your paths."* Trusting in the Lord with all my heart is having the "character of faith."

I understand that I cannot establish my own righteousness in my works by attending church and doing nice things. My walk, which is the way I live, has to match my talk. We have to walk the talk! Put up or shut up! Put your money where your mouth is! Most people don't just want to hear the sermon; they want to see it, and that is done in the way we live. My salvation has to show in the way I live and in my responses to everyday life. The day Jesus found me, I was a wreck. I had been condemned and left like an abandoned building, and it has been His job to clean me up and restore me to a useful life. He restores and rebuilds that which has been condemned because there is no condemnation in Christ Jesus. **John 3:16,** *"For God so loved the world that he gave his only Son, so that everyone who believes in him will not perish but have eternal life. God did not send his Son into the world to condemn it, but to save it."*

God has changed my character, and He continues this process. When I was using drugs, I had a passion for drugs, and I was capable of doing anything to get my drug. I did not get to that point of doing it all, but I did my fair share and some. I was capable of doing it, if it meant I could get high. Times like that I dare not forget; I am reminded of what I am capable of doing, and without God being the focus of my life, I am at high risk of repeating the cycle all over again.

One stormy winter day in 1987, Oklahoma City was covered with ice, and the weather report warned us to stay inside if it was not an emergency or extremely important to travel. When a drug addict wants his or her drug, it is always extremely important to travel, and I didn't think the weather report was for me. Hey, I had to travel because I had to get my drug! So I found another fool who was as desperate as I was and talked him into driving me to get the drugs. The trip to the dope dealer's house was dangerous enough, but when we arrived at the house, it was impossible to walk to the house without falling down on the sheet of ice that covered his yard. I slipped and fell so many times on the ice trying to get to the front door to purchase my crack cocaine until finally on the last desperate attempt I thought it would be best to stay on my hands and knees. So, I crawled like a four-legged animal up to the porch, determined to get what I needed. I refused to go back to the car until I had in my hands what I came for. I had resolved that this was not going to be a wasted trip. I remember very clearly how the drug dealer looked at me when he opened the door. Nothing could stop me now; I could not let his look stop me either. I told him with firmness, "I didn't come for a sermon; I came for only one thing. You know what it is; give it to me and let me go on my way." That was really the beginning of the end for me, demoralization.

When I look back over my life, I feel that God had to scrape the bottom of the barrel to find me. I was so lost, and I thank Him for coming to find me. Well, today I have that same passion and drive that I had to get my drug, to know God better and to be in relationship with Him. I have made a decision to put that same zeal and drive to work positively for me to live the life God meant for me. In the process, I continue to remind myself that I can do all things through Christ who strengthens me. As long as I remind myself that this life cannot be lived in my strength alone, I think I'll be just fine.

God created us to have relationships and to live in harmony with each other. In order to have successful relationships, we first need to have concern for each other and each other's needs. I believe my main reason for seeking alcohol and drugs for my fix was the lack of getting my needs met. In many ways, I have lived a selfish life; it was all about me and very seldom did I think about you. I have to maintain a consistent inspection of myself because it is easy to fall back into my old ways of doing things. I have to keep a conscious mind on how I can be a blessing to other people today. "What can I do for others today?" is a question that I need to keep with me. The Lord assures us in Matthew chapter five that those who show mercy receive mercy; this is just another Kingdom principle on how to live and treat other people.

We must get rid of the masks that hide our true selves. It is time to live life and be ourselves. It is time to be seen, not only by God and other people, but we need to see who we are. When I was high on drugs, I found living in a fantasy world was less painful than reality. I did not like myself, so it was easier to make a new person. Today, knowing who I am in Christ, I ask myself, "Why be anybody else when I am so good at being me?" God has made me an original, one of a kind, a special person with special gifts. God has enough run-of-the-mill preachers; He is looking for someone to step out of the boat and walk on water in the middle of the storm, as Peter did. God wants someone to dare to do the impossible, to step away from the norm, and to live by faith. God is able to take our little human efforts and work great miracles in our lives.

I know that my family and friends who knew me as a junkie and knew of my lifestyle are amazed at the miraculous power of God. My praises go to God because no human power could save me! I now have something in my life that is worth dying for: my relationship with Him. A man once said, "If you don't have something in your life worth dying for, it's not worth living." In this race, we die daily; we die to our old ways, and our fleshly desires that lead to eternal death, we give them up! I have stood up for so many things in my life that were not worth fighting for; now I can stand and fight for my own life and the healing of my family.

It's time to stand and fight! The armor given to us by God is protection only for the front; there is nothing for the back. We have to take a stand. As a young girl, we had a small boxer, and his name was Butch. He was the smallest dog in the neighborhood, compared to the German shepherds and other mixed hounds that would roam the area. It seemed that every time Butch would wander too far from home, the dogs would chase him home. I can recall on many accounts, Butch running with all his might to make it home, with several dogs chasing him. I was afraid for Butch if they caught him, and it appeared that Butch was afraid of what would happen too. I don't know if this became a game for Butch or not, but they never caught him. One thing I am reminded of that Butch would do each time is that he would run as fast as he could until he hit the front yard. He was running so fast it appeared that his rear end would pass his front. When I saw him coming, I would stand in the yard and beckon him on by calling his name. As soon as Butch would land on familiar ground, he would turn toward the dogs and make a stand. Even with Butch, there came a time to fight. If he didn't take a stand, he would have to keep running. We can't keep running; we have to take a stand, and it takes faith to stand. Maybe, Butch's faith was in the fact that I would protect him. When we believe that God is our "Protector and the one who fights for us, we too can stand.

Living my life with the character of faith takes my eyes off of what people say or think and puts my eyes on heavenly rewards. This is something rare; how many of us wake up in the morning with heaven on our minds? Not very often, we have to take our minds and eyes off the problems in this world and put our eyes on God. When we keep our eyes on Jesus, we can press toward the mark of the High Calling. We can make it to the finish line and become all that God has in mind for us to be, which is my desire today. While God restores us, our lives become an example for other people to follow. Others will be able to say, "If you made it through that, then so can I."

As long as we keep ourselves in check, we are able to set some things straight in our lives. With God's help, we can make those crooked roads straight again. We make sure that God has priority in our lives, and He is in His rightful place, which is first. God wants a relationship with me that's free of the distractions of my destructive addictions. With God as the center in my life, He can keep me from becoming addicted or dependent on anything else. I spent a lot of time with my addiction; it consumed my time and energy. My drug addiction took over my thought life, which dominated my actions, and I had very little time for God, if any. You can be sure that if something takes over our thoughts, "it" has us. My old destructive habits can destroy my relationship with God and ruin my life, if I allow it to go unchecked. Therefore, I keep setting things straight in my life and find healing for my mind, body, and soul.

Part of our continued healing is to protect ourselves from the seduction of this world and the temptation of the enemy. In the past, I have found my meaning, identity, security, and purpose in drugs, sex, power, work, money, drinking alcohol, pleasure, prestige, and so many other things. In this process of healing, I humble myself and ask God to do for me what I can't do for myself, but there are things I have to do in order to maintain my sobriety. I have to watch, pray, and stay alert so I'm not caught off-guard. Complacency and forgetting can make me doomed to repeat insanity. It is a valuable commodity to remember what God has delivered us from in order to continue our journey and be healed from the past.

Ask yourself these questions as you examine yourself and your own relationship with God. Are there areas you need to set straight? Where is your heart? What is it in your life that pleases you the most? Are you truly sold out to God by being completely faithful to Him? Is there another love that takes His place? Have you been so busy you have been forgetting God lately? When God is the center of our being, then we are able to love each other and live in harmony as God intended. **1 John 4:9–11,** *"God showed how much he loved us by sending his only Son into the world so that we might have eternal life through him. This is real love. It is not that we loved God, but that he loved us and sent his Son as a sacrifice to take away our sins. Dear friends, since God loved us that much, we surely ought to love each other.* **(1 John 4:16)** *We know how much God loves us, and we have put our trust in him. God is love, and all who live in love live in God, and God lives in them.* <u>And as we live in God, our love grows more perfect.</u>

We let Him fill all the emptiness in our lives, because He is the only thing that can fill that task. Love is so important to our existence because without "Love," we die. When we come to know real love (which is to have a relationship with God), we can start to change some things in our lives and set a standard of living that is pleasing to God. Keeping ourselves in check is a lifelong process. And we thank God that we don't have to act out our thoughts!

CHAPTER ELEVEN
"STAY CONNECTED"

Ephesians 3:17: "May Christ through your faith actually dwell, settle down, abide, make his permanent home in your hearts. May you be rooted deep in love and founded securely on Love."

I have to stay connected, stay hooked up to the body of Christ. It is very important to my recovery and my healing to stay in contact with other believers in the family of God. It is even more important to stay connected to God, and that is done through prayer, fellowship, and reading His Word. Keep in mind that those who isolate themselves from God and His family and try to go it alone cut themselves off from God's power. The most dangerous and unsafe place to be is out of God's protection, out of fellowship with Him, or out of His will for us.

If you can imagine vacuuming a floor, and when you move the sweeper out so far along the floor from the plug, you can disconnect the power. Even though you can continue on in the process of vacuuming without the "power," you are only going through the motion. Without the "Power," we are only going through the "imitation" of life. God wants our lives to be more than just going through the motion. We have to stay connected to the "Power" and make sure not to move too far away from our power source. It's God's power working through us that gives us the courage, strength, and right words to say. John chapter fifteen says that Jesus loves us: "I have loved you even as the Father has loved me. Remain in my love." We have plugged into many things before, looking for that quick fix—drugs, sex, food, and money—only to be disappointed time after time. Jesus is our connection to a full life. But we have to connect by knowing the scripture and knowing the power of God.

My recovery suggests that I cannot stay sober alone, and I can do nothing without God in my life. He is my power source. It's really simple; in order to have power, you have to stay hooked up to the Higher Power. We can stay hooked up by prayer, faith, obedience, and trust. Our confidence comes about, because of our great <u>trust</u> in God through Christ. It is not that we think we can do anything of lasting value by ourselves. Our only <u>power</u> and success come from God.

In **John 14:1–8,** Jesus says, *"I am the true vine, and my Father is the gardener. Remain in me, and I will remain in you. For a branch cannot* *produce fruit if it is severed from the vine, and you cannot be fruitful apart from me. Yes, I am the vine, you are the branches. Those who remain in me, and I in them, will produce much fruit. For apart from me you can do nothing. But if you stay joined to me and my words remain in you, you may ask any request you like, and it will be granted!"* What power we have just by staying connected to Jesus! We can ask what we want, and it will be granted, because we are asking in His will.

My life experiences have brought me to my rightful position before the Lord, one of humility and prayer. In the beginning of my recovery, I struggled with the concept of a surrendered life. My understanding and my thinking was an enemy to God, and I was so afraid of God's will and what He wanted for me that I could not imagine giving Him control of my life. It was obvious that there was the existence of two distinct "wills" (mine and God's). He said, "Yes," and I said, "No." And through my process of healing, our wills have merged together, bringing us into harmony and relationship. Miraculously, what I want for me is what God wants for me, and what God wants for me is what I want for me. One thing for sure, I know He doesn't want me high on drugs and alcohol. Furthermore, His will for me is to stop hurting myself. God is a love greater than myself and a love greater than my addiction, and my healing continues by staying connected to that love. When I stay connected, I have to wait upon the Lord and allow Him to direct my path. At this position in my life, I know that God's will for me is best.

During most of my life, especially in my active addiction, I was lost; therefore, my heart and mind worked against each other. My mind would come up with some bright idea, and my heart would try to talk me out of it by saying, "You don't want to do that." My flesh would win over since it was the strongest at the time because I fed it most often. Now because of Christ's Redemption, I am no longer a slave to sin. **Romans 6:14,** *"Sin is no longer your master, for you are no longer subject to the law, which enslaves you to sin. Instead, you are free by God's grace."* **2 Corinthians 2:6,** *"He is the one who has enabled us to represent his new covenant. This is a covenant, not of written laws, but of the Spirit. The old way ends in death; in the new way, the Holy Spirit gives life."*

I have compromised my morals and values long enough, which has always led to shame and guilt as well as low self-esteem. I can honestly say that my best plan in my active addiction almost killed me. My "will" was definitely not God's will for me. One of my greatest plans in my addiction was to sell enough cocaine and get rich quickly and quit. Well, that didn't work either, because I was addicted to my own product. My plans to get rich quickly changed to the thought, "If I could use enough cocaine, it would kill me, and I would not have to keep living this way." I don't believe I was truly suicidal at that time, but I did think that if I used enough dope I would float out of here peacefully. I didn't want a messy or painful ending.

Furthermore, I thought God could not possibly love me because of the things I was doing and the things I had done. I merely existed, occupying a space I thought someone else could make better use of. At or near the end of my drug use, around the age of twenty-nine, I found myself alone, and my days consisted of smoking cocaine, isolated, crying in pain. If you want to see pain, find an active drug addict. I can now look back and see that I was sitting on the sidelines of life watching the entire world prepare for heaven and letting it pass me by. The world around me appeared to be preparing for something better, something I believed was unattainable for me, and regretfully, I was not connected to anything but my drug. It was my one and true relationship.

The only thing that set me free was the truth, and that truth is Jesus! Yes, the truth will set you free, but it will piss you off first! The truth is confrontive; Jesus confronted the Pharisees' false behavior all the time. Jesus is the way, the truth, and the life. We can live any way we choose to and believe what we want because everything in this world is permissible. The day will come when everyone will come face to face with the "Truth," and it will still be up to the individual whether he or she accepts it or not. We all have our own so-called "come-to-Jesus meeting" scheduled in this life. The fact is that there is only one way to freedom; there is only one way to God the Father, and that is through Christ Jesus. And we all need our own personal relationship with Him. This relationship is not something that can be borrowed at the last minute to suffice; we develop it and build on it by connecting to God and staying connected.

We can stay united with God through prayer and meditating on His goodness and His power. Prayer is not a way for us to control God; it is a way for us to put ourselves under His control and ponder on all the things He has done for us. When I made the decision to stay sober and give up drugs, I had to pray daily that the Lord would keep me sober. Sometimes I had to take each day moment by moment because the days seem so impossibly long. Through prayer and holy meditation, I have been able to improve my relationship and tête-à-tête with God. This has increased my peace with His will being done in my life. The connection to God gives us the power to carry out His will for us because, I can't say it enough, "We can't do it alone!" And thank God we are not without "Hope"!

Pride can keep us isolated from God, because with pride we think we don't need help. Pride is evident before the destruction. I know what it feels like to be hopeless and feel overwhelmed by troubles that are caused by addiction and life. But since "Hope" came into my life, all I have to do is cry out to God, and He will hear me because He made a promise that He will always hear me. It is comforting to know without a doubt that God is listening to my prayers. God's children have an advantage because we have the Word of God. The Bible enlightens us about God; it gives us insight about His character and about His power to help us if we stay connected to Him. No situation is hopeless for those who call out to God. I cried out to Him from the bottom of my despair, and He heard me! I cried out to Him during my divorce, and He heard me! I cried out to Him in the middle of abuse and losses, and He still heard me!

God heard me because His love is unfailing. He is faithful to His Word, in spite of us. Not only did God hear me, He answered me. God listens to our cries for help, and He is there to pull us out of whatever trap we are in. The psalmists in the Bible are my favorite because they cried out in their misery; they did it all. They admitted their sins to God, voiced their doubts, told God of their fears, and asked God for help in the middle of their storms or pressures in life. The psalmists praised God and worshiped Him regardless of their circumstances. No matter what the circumstance, they always shared honest feelings with God. This is an example for us to live by, and it has given me reassurance during my times of struggle and pain. God wants that genuine, real, and honest communication with us that breeds intimacy. There is no need in going to Him with any superficial conversation because He knows us; He made us. When we can cry out to God like the psalmist did, without holding back, being honest with Him, knowing that He hears our prayers, and believing He will answer, circumstances will change. Paul is another that was not moved by his circumstances. Although locked in prison, he made it his business to stay connected to the Lord and let the world know that he was not a prisoner to man but a prisoner of Jesus Christ.

The Bible says that God knows everything about us. So, why try to fool Him? We can fool others and may even fool ourselves, but we can never fool God. He knows our hearts because He has searched us and He made us. He may not direct all my thoughts and words since we have free will, but He knows all my choices. He knows us through and through. He knows our successes, our failures, and where it will end for us. In addition, there is nowhere we can go that He is not there. This just shows His omnipotence and omnipresence. We are His people and the sheep of His pastures. Most of all, Jesus knows our grief; He is very much acquainted with grief and anguish.

We stay connected to God by meditating, thinking, and reflecting on how good He is in our lives, and this can take us through any storm. There are times we just have to do a simple gratitude list and meditate on the things in our lives that we can be grateful about. I have to will myself to concentrate on the many reasons I have to be happy. When I think of where God has brought me from to this point, my soul cries with joy. I have given up the identity of "crack head" and received my new title as the "daughter of the King." As we depend on God, it strengthens our faith walk and gives us the power to carry out the healing process in our lives.

Stay connected to God! He alone can fill us and satisfy us in ways we have always searched for. I have tried to fill myself up on various things, but they were usually temporary and made things worse. God is my satisfaction today; He has truly changed my life. I know that I have been changed! When we meditate on God, He can change us. He can take our focus off the problem and put it on Him where it belongs.

My God is the God who brought His people out of slavery into the promised land, and He will do the same for us. Most of us have lived in slavery, and some are still living in slavery even with a Savior. This book is for you too. What bondage is in your life? It may not be drug addiction, but what is it? Whatever the case, God can bring us out of bondage into freedom, out of addictions into freedom. He is the God of deliverance. God will not only bring us out of bad situations, but He will take us into the blessings, into the promised land. God always takes us into something much better than what He brought us out of. He is so awesome! Psalms 77:16 says that when the Red Sea saw God, its waters looked and shivered with fear! The Red Sea is symbolic to any obstacle or impossible problem in our lives. The Red Sea seemed impossible for the children of Israel and Moses, but it was only an opportunity for God to do what He does best. Our problems that arise are just opportunities for God's power to be demonstrated in our lives. In order for us to pass through our problems or conquer them, we have to introduce our obstacles or problems to the Holy God and watch them split! God is the God that even the winds of the storm obey.

God can show us a path out of our problems that no one else knows is there. As we have heard, if He brought you to it, He will take you through it. God wants us saved and delivered. My life and recovery process has been like a carpenter sanding and trimming the rough edges of a piece of wood, preparing his work for use. He doesn't change the grain of wood; he just smoothes it out. Jesus is definitely the master craftsman. Just as God removed His people from Egypt (slavery), He had to remove the mentality of slavery from the people. Many times, we can be free physically, but our thinking holds us captive. God can show us how to exchange our slavery ways of living and thinking. We can take control of our thought life by shaking loose any thought that comes against the will of God in our lives. We renew our minds through the Word of God, and the Holy Spirit stands guard over our thought life.

Our communication with God keeps us connected. Prayer is part of the communication that keeps us connected to the Father through Jesus Christ. When Jesus died, He opened up the way for us to go boldly to the Father. When I pray, it is a personal conversation with God. I'm past the point of trying to make an impression on whoever is listening by saying the right words. Our relationship is too important; my gratitude toward God is too important to waste time with meaningless words.

The more we pray, the better or stronger our connection becomes with God. He said, "My sheep know my voice." Without the constant effort of communication with God, we cannot become familiar with His voice. His ears are open to our prayers because He is a God that not only hears our prayers but answers them too.

We stay connected by being consistent and persistent in our efforts; we can't give up. Although sometimes it might seem easier to give up, we have to stay connected. We know that God rewards those who are persistent and diligent in seeking Him. We are connected because of His promises. God doesn't take back His Word, so we operate out of the promised word, not our feelings. Our feelings are subject to change at any moment. Keep in mind that God is with us even when we cannot feel Him. We know it simply because He said so. God made us a promise that He would never leave us or forsake us. So our job is to stay close to Him, to not disconnect ourselves by turning to other gods in our lives. He is our only satisfaction. **Psalms 63:56** says in speaking of God, *"You satisfy me more than the richest of foods. I will praise you with songs of joy. I will awake thinking of you, meditating on you through the night."* **Now, that's staying connected!**

CHAPTER TWELVE
"STEPPIN' WITH CHRIST"

Isaiah 61:1–3, *"The Spirit of the Sovereign Lord is upon me, because that Lord has appointed me to bring good news to the poor. He has sent me to comfort the brokenhearted and to announce that captives will be released and prisoners will be freed. He has sent me to tell those who mourn that the time of the LORD'S favor has come, and with it, the day of God's anger against their enemies. To all who mourn in Israel, he will give beauty for ashes, joy instead of mourning, praise instead of despair. For the LORD has planted them like strong and graceful oaks for his own glory."*

The message I have is one of "Hope." The message I carry to those who are suffering and enslaved to their fleshly desires is that "You don't have to die in the midst of your addiction, if you don't want to." My desire is that God can speak a word of freedom through me. I know that I did not go through everything I have experienced to just do nothing, because that would make all my life experiences in vain, and Jesus' dying for me would be in vain—with no purpose.

Jesus is looking for a servant's heart to carry an effective message of life through the way we live—as when He chose His disciples, not from power and prestige, but from their hearts. Jesus knows our hearts so we can stop the manipulation of the appearance of humility. The greatest position we can have is one of a servant. Greatness comes from serving and giving of ourselves to help God and others. Jesus' life here on earth went against what the world thinks is power. The world sees power as a way to gain control over others. But Jesus, who had all power in His hands, came to earth and chose to serve others. He washed the dirty feet of his disciples and hung out with the "less thans" and died that bloody death on the cross for our sins. So, "steppin' with Christ" is to hang out with Him, learn His ways and copy His ways in our lives. The power message is that He got up. Many great men and women have died; many gods that are worshiped have died, but only one is known to have risen, and that is our Lord Jesus.

Jesus said, "Go into the world and preach the Good News of salvation, that there is an eternal way out from the bondage and penalty of sin." Jesus said to preach this message to everyone. **Romans 10:14–15,** *"But how can they call on him to save them unless they believe in him? And how* *can they believe in him if they have never heard about him? And how can they hear about him unless someone tells them? And how will anyone go and tell them without being sent? That is what the Scriptures mean when they say, 'How beautiful are the feet of those who bring good news!'"* God wants us to tell it! To tell our story to whoever will listen. Our power to tell it comes in knowing Christ. The more I learn about Jesus, the freer I get in my mind. **Mark 16:13,** *(Jesus appears to two believers traveling on the road) "When they realized who he was, they rushed back to tell the others, but no one believed them."* When we have a spiritual awakening, we come to realize God's power. There is a great difference in knowing Him and knowing about Him. See, it's not enough to read about Christ; we have to believe that He is God, trust Him to save us, and accept Him as LORD! When we come to know Him, then He can use us to help others because we are <u>motivated</u> to share with others what He has done for us. He will give us opportunities and the inner strength to tell His message.

God wants to use us. He said to me, "Let me use your voice to *comfort the brokenhearted, announce that captives will be released and prisoners will be freed. I want to tell those who mourn that the time of the Lord's favor has come and with it the day of God's anger against their enemies. I want to tell my people who mourn that I will give beauty for ashes, joy instead of mourning, and praise instead of despair."* In this, God will get the glory, because all will know that it had to be Him who carried us through. While carrying God's message, we stay in step with the Holy Spirit. God changes our thinking, and those who are controlled by the Holy Spirit think about the things that please the Spirit (Rom. 8:5).

If we are to live by the Spirit, we are to keep in step with the Spirit. Steppin' with Christ comes only by being directed by the Holy Spirit. Throughout all my trials and experiences, God has been preparing me for service, and it has been a long and painful journey and training. I enlisted in the army of God and became a soldier for the Lord when I accepted Jesus into my life to guide and direct me. I am a follower of Jesus Christ, and a follower is a spiritual soldier.

Therefore, soldiers have to go into training to be ready for battle. God has to equip us to carry His message to those who are suffering. A good soldier has to be taught how to take a blow and continue to stand. The devil will throw stuff at us to see how well we're suited. If we are suited, no matter what life throws at us, we can triumph because we are free in Christ. We have to put on the full armor of God that we may be able to stand in times of troubles and adversities (Ephesians chapter six).

When God saves us, we may become the only Bible that some people may see in their lives, and they have to be able to see the love of God in us. God's love transforms lives, changes the hardest hearts, quiets the storms, and changes attitudes. **2 Corinthians 2:14–17,** *"But thanks be to God, who made us his captives and leads us along in Christ's triumphal procession. Now wherever we go he uses us to tell others about the Lord and to spread the Good News like a sweet perfume. Our lives are a fragrance presented by Christ to God. But this fragrance is perceived differently by those being saved and by those perishing. To those who are perishing we are a fearful smell of death and doom. But to those who are being saved we are a life-giving perfume. And who is adequate for such a task as this? You see, we are not like those hucksters and there are many of them—who preach just to make money. We preach God's message with sincerity and with Christ's authority. And we know that the God who sent us is watching us."*

I can clearly see that my life experience has been for someone else. I am an overcomer, and my experiences are designed to pull someone else out of bondage, hoping that he or she can pull someone out too. God uses people to testify on His mighty power to offer hope. We break the chain of addiction and bondage by finding freedom in Christ, allowing Him to heal us, and healing involves pain. God's provision of healing sometimes happens in <u>steps</u> that come together to make a whole life.

As I reflect back over my life, I know that the devil meant me no good, and he (devil) is still looking for what he can steal, kill, and destroy in my life. But at the same time, God is working things out for the good of those who love the Lord and those who are in a relationship with Him. We move past salvation to transformation, the process of healing. When Jesus is active in our lives, there is a change, sometimes quickly, sometimes slowly, but the most important fact is that a change takes place.

Victory usually comes after pain and tears (no pain, no gain). We remember that weeping may endure for a night, but joy comes in the morning. There is comfort in knowing that whatever you find yourself going through, it too shall pass! Many trials have come, and they have gone.

My spirit has been awakened. I was once dead inside, and now I live. Where I was once dying in sin, I now live in Christ. My old nature died, and now Christ lives in me. After our dead spirits have been awakened from the dark and introduced to the "Light," we have had a spiritual awakening, which is a change of our attitude and how we see this world. As I went through my adolescent years and young adulthood, including my addiction, I heard one comment quite often, and that was, "You need to change your attitude!" I thought everybody else had the attitude that needed adjusting, and that's just how I would respond! So as I tore through life, fighting, getting fired from jobs, getting married and divorced, etc., I kept hearing, "You need to change your attitude!" Well, when I arrived at my first support group meeting, beaten from life and my drug addiction, they told me what I needed most of all was an attitude change! It was over, all the running I did, and I still could not get past the fact that what I needed most of all was an attitude change, which is nothing less than a spiritual awakening. God has a purpose to be fulfilled in this world and in our lives, and it will be done.

The apostle Paul tells us in Galatians 5:16 to live according to our new life in the Holy Spirit. We do this as a result of God cleansing us and drawing us closer to Him. My spirit has been awakened, and I have been given the strength to not do what my old destructive sinful nature wants me to. I don't have to use drugs today if I don't want to; it's now a simple choice, a choice I didn't know I had when I was using cocaine. I thought I had to use no matter what. Our choices can lead to bondage or freedom; the healthier we are, the healthier our choices become. As I look back at the things I used to do and say, it feels sometimes that it wasn't me. What a wonderful job God has done! I no longer sleep!

We awaken our spirit by feeding it. If we digest God's Word, we feed our spirit man. We give the Word more than a glance or peek. We don't just read it during Sunday service as we follow along with the minister. We digest God's Word on a daily basis. God's message must sink deep into our heart and show in our actions before we can effectively help others understand and apply the Gospel. **Ezekiel 3:1–4,** *"The voice said to me, 'Son of man, eat what I am giving you—eat this scroll! Then go and give its message to the people of Israel.' So I opened my mouth, and he fed me the scroll. 'Eat it all,' he said. And when I ate it, it tasted as sweet as honey. Then he said, 'Son of man, go to the people of Israel with my messages.'"* The Word of God says, "Oh taste and see that the Lord is good!"

I want others to see the love of God as I am seeing it! When I tried cocaine the first time, I wanted everyone I knew to try it because it was so good! I carried a deadly message, because cocaine made me feel like I was home; I had arrived! I thought I was at a point in my personal being where I always wanted to be. The euphoria, the promise that cocaine made me was awesome! The feeling was far above what I could ever imagine. I remember saying, "Wow! This is how I always wanted to feel": sexy, happy, free, confident, etc. ... Oh, but at the end of my addiction, cocaine turned on me like a vicious dog! It stole from me and lied to me. Our love affair ended! My addiction left me at a point of eyeing the slop in my life, thinking and justifying how I could live with it. But God was not finished with me!

God is not finished until the world can see His power. He said every knee shall bow and every tongue must confess that Jesus Christ is the Son of God. He is not finished until His Glory can be seen. Our mission as Christians was passed on to us by Jesus. The Gospel is not something to keep concealed or closed off from others; it is something to share. We don't have to be jealous; there is enough Jesus for everyone to get equal portions. The Gospel is not something we merely ponder or debate; it has to be proclaimed, to be made known, to be spread to the world! And without God's grace and help, we could never carry out His plan and do His work. Most of us need favor in our lives anyway; God's grace shows us favor in situations we know we do not deserve. His grace covers us even in our mistakes, our shortcomings, and our humanism.

We are to tell our stories, show our gratitude, and give our testimonies about what God has done for us or how He delivered us from hopeless situations; this is carrying a message of "Hope." **Galatians 6:1,** *"Dear brothers and sisters, if another Christian is overcome by some sin, you who are godly should gently and humbly help that person back into the right path. And be careful not to fall into the same temptation yourself. If you think you are too important to help someone in need, you are only fooling yourself. You are really a nobody."*

We show our confidence and acceptance in God by the way we live; it is our gift back to Him for saving us, even though we can never repay Him. Part of carrying God's message is to meet the need; we are sensitive to the need of others with the guidance of the Holy Spirit. He equips us to meet the need. In Acts 1:8, Jesus says, *"But when the Holy Spirit comes upon you, you will receive power, power to tell people about Me everywhere."* With the power of the Holy Spirit, we are to share the good news of salvation through Christ, which makes us free not to use drugs anymore. I am not ashamed; the devil will tell us that we have nothing to say. But I have a power living in me that has something to say, so who is man that I shall be mindful of him or intimidated by him? And after this trial of life is all done, I want to hear those famous words, "Well done, my good and <u>faithful</u> servant."

When God judges us on our deeds and motives, He will say, "You met the need of my people," or "You didn't meet the need of my people." "When I was hungry, you fed me; when I was thirsty, you gave me something to drink; when I was sick, you came to see about me" (this is meeting the need). We use the knowledge given to us by the Holy Spirit to make wise decisions; we don't want to give clothing to someone who needs food just to say we did a good deed. We don't want to just take on the appearance of God without the knowledge. **Romans 10:2–4,** *"I know that enthusiasm* *they have for God, but it is misdirected zeal. For they don't understand God's way of making people right with himself. Instead, they are clinging to their own way of getting right with God by trying to keep the law. They won't go along with God's way. For Christ has accomplished the whole purpose of the law. All who believe in him are made right with God."* Good deeds will not save us, but they can show, when coupled with a good heart, that we have accepted the love of God. If we cannot show love to others, maybe we have not accepted the love of our Father. If we cannot show mercy to others, maybe we have not accepted the mercy of our Father. When we face death, can we say that the world is a better place because of us? If not, we need to start today with the focus of how we can improve the quality of someone else's life by improving our own.

After all that God has done for me, it is an honor to carry His message; it is an honor for me to give back to Him. I know I can never repay Christ for the debt He paid on my behalf, but I can give back; I can pay on the account, and that in itself is gratifying. I am the only one who really knows how far God has brought me. I hope this book has revealed to you what God did to rescue me, even when it appeared that it was a job that could not be done. It was only a job for El-Shaddai, the Almighty God, because nothing is too big for God! He is the restorer of my faith! He is restoring my soul as He promised; there is no better place to be than to be with God. Although I may walk through the valley and shadow of death, I will fear no evil, because God is with me and He comforts me. I have tried this world, and the things it has to offer are only temporary and lead to destruction. During my addiction, I lost me; my life was one big crazy party, a wild storm, and God calmed the madness in my life.

I was a hopeless drug addict who would do anything to get what I wanted, and God picked me up, cleaned me up, and set me high upon a "Rock." That rock is Jesus! What He did for me, He will do for you. My whole life today is centered on helping someone else get set free by finding freedom in Christ Jesus. No! I have not arrived, but I thank God I am not what I used to be. I thank God that I am not where I used to be. He was the way out of my life of bondage; He is the only way out of bondage! Addiction cannot hold you when you have Jesus and His Holy Spirit working to guide and protect you. The devil is no match for Jesus, and by the way, if you don't know it, in the end when it is all said and done, the devil loses!

Until then, we have work to do, because the devil is always looking for someone to bamboozle into his tricks; he wants to take as many as he can with him to hell! When we are steppin' with Christ we are living with Christ in our lives; He is the manager and ruler in our lives. He makes it so we will not be fooled by the devil, because God supplies us with the truth. We spread that truth, and Jesus is made evident to others by the way we live. We don't want to live a life that contradicts what we say or who we say we are. I don't want to say only in my words that "Jesus is the only way," and my life dictates the opposite.

We live in a world where there are so many temptations and empty promises. People are making promises with no true intentions to carry them out or fulfill them. (Is the whole world on drugs?) The devil uses our temptations; whatever our flesh desires is what he will make readily available to us. But God gives us a way out of all our temptations. **1 Corinthians 10:13,** *"But remember that the temptations that come into your life are no different from what others experience. And God is faithful. He will keep the temptation from becoming so strong that you can't stand up against it. When you are tempted, he will show you a way out so that you will not give in to it."*

Our nation alone spends billions of dollars a year on advertisements or, can I say, making promises. For billions of dollars, they promise to make our lives better and make us happier. I have often wondered how much is spent on making sure the promises are fulfilled. Jesus is God's offering or payment to make sure His promise was fulfilled.

The variety of advertisements that devour our lives promise us all kinds of pleasures, fulfillments, and improvements in our lives, but you know as well as I do in the end we don't quite get what we have been promised. The delicious food when delivered to the table doesn't exactly look like the commercial. Know that God is a promise keeper, His words are not empty, and they do not return to Him void, but filled with "yes" and "amen."

Living with Christ goes past empty words into action. The action continues with gratitude for what God has done and what He can do. Hold on to your promises! If you don't have a promise, read the Word of God, He will reveal His promises to you. Receive His promises today! Jesus was a promise from God, a promise to send us a Savior. Jesus is God's promise fulfilled; receive God's promise today!

"Father, as I look over my life, I just want to say thank you!"

Psalms 107, *"Give thanks to the Lord, for he is good! His faithful love endures forever. Has the Lord redeemed you? Then speak out! Tell others he has saved you from your enemies."* Not only do people need to hear the Word of God, they also need to hear how He has worked in our lives. Others develop hope from our stories. There are many ministers, preachers, leaders, and pastors who stand before the people each Sunday, and it appears as if they have not experienced any hard times or trials. I tried to go to church during my addiction; I was looking for someone who understood, and none of those people looked like I was feeling. Well, that could be the miracle-working power of God in their lives, or they could be hiding. Whatever the case, I believe that if others are not able to see what we have been through, it is our duty, as Paul did, to tell them and let them know how far God has brought us. Hey, don't get me wrong; I am grateful today that when people look at me, they no longer see me as a "crack head"! It only means that God is good at what He does! I don't want to just talk, but lead somebody to Christ with the way I live. I am willing, able, and capable to tell it! I have noticed that when I tell my story, it's hard for some to believe that it is not boasting, just restoration! Hallelujah!

God's healing power can change us so that people won't recognize us. In **John 9:1–11,** Jesus heals a man born blind, but *"His neighbors and others who knew him as a blind beggar asked each other, 'Is this the same man—that beggar?'"* (verse 8). *"Some said he was, and others said, o, but surely looks like him!' and the beggar kept saying, 'I am that man.' They asked, 'Who healed you? What happened?'"* (verse 9). His answer was Jesus. Jesus is what happened to me! I am not the same!

God uses people to perform His great works. He has used somebody to pull me out of my despair, and my job is to pull somebody else out. That person will pull somebody out, and when we look back, we will see an endless line of people being pulled out of the slavery to freedom. We overcome by the blood of the lamb and the word of our testimony (Rev. 12:11).

I thank God today for my sobriety, my husband, my family, my children, my mother, and especially my grandchildren, who have never seen me high. God gave me my responsibilities back. I thank God for how far He has brought me and for the many blessings in my life today. I thank Him for the transformation in my life. He took someone like me, so messed up, and made me fit. I know where I fit today; I am a child of God! A daughter of the King! I have "Hope" today. I attend support group meetings because God is changing me every day. And He said in **Hebrews 10:25,** *"And let us not neglect our meeting together, as some people do, but encourage and warn each other, especially now that the day of his coming back again is drawing near."* I can't stay sober and maintain this way of life on my own; I need you!

Relationships are important to God and through this healing process of recovery, He has mended, restored, and given me new relationships that I could of never imagined. I thank God for two important and dear friends that He has given me, Gloria Martin and Marylina Thornton. I love you both and I will keep in my heart all of the many experiences that we have had through this journey.

One other paradox of this way of life is that "I can't keep what I have unless I give it away." I have surrendered to the process. **Today I am free and I belong! Today I am Steppin' with Christ.** My view of life has changed. When we step with Christ, we begin to see this world through His eyes. Steppin' with Christ means to hang out with Him, learn His ways, and copy His ways in all that we do. It is the only way for me to survive because there is something wrong with the way I see things. If I stay with Him, He will renew my thoughts each day; each day, I am recovering. Today, I do not regret my past, nor do I wish to shut the door on it! Many cannot be healed from their hurts because of the regret and shame that is involved. I realize how my experiences can benefit others. Someone will need to know that God can reach our lowest points in our lives and snatch us out! Yes, there is a way out of addiction; there is a way out of the bondage that holds us as slaves. And yes, HEALING HURTS, but it is a hurt that heals! Jesus is our Healing; it is through Him that we are healed. **Where does it hurt?** Give that hurt to God and let Him through His miracle-working power heal your hurts!